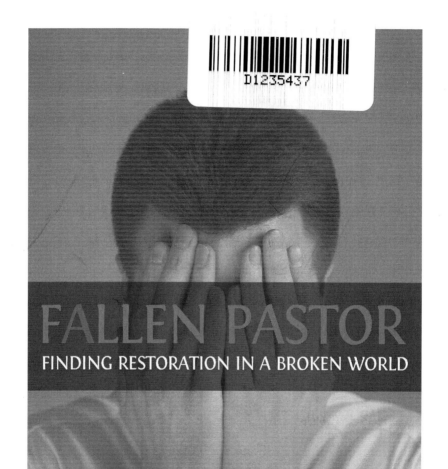

FALLEN PASTOR

FINDING RESTORATION IN A BROKEN WORLD

Copyright Notice

FALLEN PASTOR

Finding Restoration in a Broken World

By Ray Carroll

CivitasPress

Publishing inspiring and redemptive ideas.[sm]

Endorsements

In sharing his own story, as well as the stories of others in ministry who have experienced similar circumstances, Ray Carroll's book accomplishes more than a simple retelling of difficult life events. This book challenges anyone in ministry to look deeply at their own lives to discover if they are headed down a similar path of these who have shared their story. The book challenges ministry families to determine if they are growing together or growing apart, and causes them to think about what they must do in order to survive the challenges of ministry. Churches also receive a challenge, because often we don't know how we should feel or behave when a minister falls. Whether you are serving in the ministry, or serving as a member of the body of Christ, and whether you are one who needs forgiveness or needs to express forgiveness, I pray this book has a profound impact on bringing both holiness and healing into the life of the body of Christ. - Dr. Randy Johnson, Senior Pastor of Florida Blvd. Baptist Church, Baton Rouge, LA.

~~

Our nation is losing pastors at and alarming rate and Ray Carroll is on a mission to change that statistic. Two weeks after Ray fell from ministry, he ran into a former church member in public. She asked him, "Why, Brother Ray - why did you do it?" Her question was sincere but full of hurt as she searched for answers - he had no answer to give. Ray addresses the fundamental question - why do pastors fall? But, he goes further. He not only answers the why, but why not. Ray's experience and research as a fallen pastor has given him insights that I am convinced are transformational for anyone in full time ministry. *Fallen Pastor: Finding Restoration in a Broken World* should be on your must read list. - Rodney Cox, founder of Ministry insights

~~

I have read many books over the past few years, and this book, quite frankly, is the most important book I have read in a very long time. *Fallen Pastor* is a book that should be handed out to every seminary/Bible college student, or anyone that is in ministry. Scratch that, every adult should read this book. Just because you don't speak from a pulpit, doesn't mean you won't be tempted. - Mike Levitt, Random Ideas Book Review

~~

There are some things in life we'd rather not talk about or even think about. Pastors falling into adultery is one of them. Yet, our silence and fear keep us from confronting a crucial subject for the church today. Ray Carroll speaks boldly, biblically, and vulnerably, sharing his own failure as a pastor as well as what he has learned as a result. He presents case studies from many "fallen pastors," as well as biblical counsel for pastors and churches. Ray challenges pastors to examine their hearts and their lives, even to admit that their church just might be their first "mistress." He challenges churches to relate to their pastors in ways that are healthy and theologically solid. This book opens up a conversation we desperately need to have if the church and her leaders are going to be whole and effective conduits of the gospel of Jesus Christ. - Dr. Mark D. Roberts, Senior Advisor and Theologian-in-Residence, Foundations for Laity Renewal, Kerrville, Texas

~~

A timely, redemptive book. While taking full responsibility for his sexual sin, Ray shares how the stress of maintaining a perfect image in a "be all/do all" job can lead to a pastor's burn out and moral failure. He calls churches to lay aside unrealistic expectations, and offer personal and job support to their leaders, plus forgiveness and reconciliation if they fall. - Joy Wilson, author of *Uncensored Prayer: the Spiritual Practice Of Wresting With God,* and a pastor's daughter.

to Allison,

my love, my beautifully complex woman.

Contents

Acknowledgements

A lot of people helped make this work possible and without them, I would neither be the man I am today nor be able to put this book into publication. There are some I am sure I will forget, so apologies in advance, but thanks to all I have spoken to and begged for help.

Many experts have given freely of their time in the writing of this book. Not only did they grant me an interview, they fed my soul: Dr. Hershael York, preaching professor at The Southern Baptist Theological Seminary; Jake Larson, co-founder of Fireproof Ministries and XXXChurch.com; Rodney Cox, CEO of Ministry Insights, who has also provided a discount coupon at the end of this book for his company's ministry profile; Dr. Bill Leonard, Director of Ministerial Care for the Church of God International Offices; Troy Haas, who oversees the care of fallen pastors each year; Roger Barrier, founder of Preach It, Teach It, senior teaching pastor of Casas Church in Tucson, Arizona, and author; Rev. Dr. Mark D. Roberts, pastor, retreat leader and author of several books including, "No Holds Barred: Wrestling With God," and "Dare to Be True"; Dr. Kaila Edger, psychiatrist and author of "Losing the Bond with God: Sexual Addiction and Evangelical Men"; Steve Reed, author of "Transformed by Tough Times"; David Trotter, author of "Lost and Found: Finding Myself by Getting Lost in an Affair"; and Michael Todd Wilson, co-founder of the Intimacy Counseling Center in Suwanee, Georgia and author of "Preventing Ministry Failure."

Thank you to my pastor, Jimmy Stewart, and Salem Baptist Church in Pembroke, Kentucky. You chose to walk with me after I fell, opening yourself to criticism. You looked beyond that and showed us love, compassion and friendship and I will always be grateful to you.

My father once told me to find people I want to be like and admire and become friends with them. My editor, Jonathan Brink, found me. He has been patient and caring toward me. More than that, he has shown me that I have a voice and even in the midst of many struggles, I have much to share.

I love Muhlenberg County, the place where I am employed. My friends in that community loved me after my fall for who I was. Thank you to all my friends, the athletes and coaches who were patient as I wrote. I especially want to thank Shelby Cotton and Lisa Hope of Muhlenberg Community Hospital for their understanding as I wrote. Thank you to Steve Smith for the promotional photography.

Aunt Cindy, thank you for never turning your back on me, for always loving me and never giving up on me. I want to be you when I grow up. To grandma and grandpa, thank you for loving me for who I am, never doubting me. I want to have a marriage like yours. To my sister and your family, thank you for being you.

Thank you to Abigail and Katie, my daughters. They have been patient as I wrote and constantly asked, "Are you done with that book yet?" You are resilient children who have endured more than your share of trouble in this life and you still act like princesses. Your daddy loves you. To their mother, thank you for allowing me to take the pain of what happened and turn it into a ministry for others. For Leslie, my stepdaughter, you're just learning to read and don't understand all the things that have happened, but I love you dearly.

To my Mom, who I'm sure would have envisioned a different topic for my first book. But I carry a piece of her in my heart always and am forever indebted to her. I have no doubt she would have been the first one to grab a copy, read it through then say, "I'm proud of you, Son."

Allison, while I wrote, you saw my highs and lows. You saw my dream and believed with me. I am proud to have you as my wife and love you with all I have. Thank you for believing in me.

To my Savior. While I pastored, I took you for granted. When I fell, I found myself cast to your feet. You were the only one between me and many. I now know what it means when the bible says, "nothing can separate us from the love of Christ."

Lastly, to all the fallen pastors I have corresponded with in the past two years. I think of you and your journey daily. When we talked, we connected on a personal level. Even if your story is not included, know that it is now part of my heart. I pray that this book will be a combined effort on all our parts to help those who have fallen, to bring the issues to light, and to keep others from experiencing the same.

Soli Deo Gloria

Foreword

After talking with Ray about his story and his desire to help others I am excited to participate in such a critical project. Nearly ten years ago now we started an organization called XXXchurch.com. Our mission is to bring awareness, prevention, and recovery to this area of sexual integrity and specifically pornography. At XXXchurch.com we work daily with individuals and families that have experienced the heartbreak and devastation of a fallen pastor. When most people have turned away from the fallen pastor we extend our hands. Doesn't Jesus invite the sinner to spend time with him? An invitation by Jesus in the midst of sin is hope for a new future. Over the last 10 years of XXXchurch.com we have escorted the fallen pastor to rehab, to intervention, to counseling, to confession, and in a few cases to prison.

Every pastor we work with wonders why they chose to make such a deadly decision. Many look at their families and feel immediate repentance and sorrow for the pain they have caused. As their family walks out the door the pain and burden of their choices sinks deep into their troubled hearts. Is there really life after the fall? Is it possible for God to forgive me after I have denied his existence through my actions?

With nearly half of all pastors admitting a regular struggle with pornography, we must address solutions to this epidemic. What practices, habits, and steps become prevalent before the fall? Can I identify habits in my life that are building a higher probability of failure in my sexual integrity? How can I rebuild my life on a foundation that will stand up against sin and stand for God?

I have been a pastor for the last 15 years and know first hand the intensity of sexual integrity. It feels like the attack for our souls through sex is elevated to epic proportions today. I can admit that without the right friendships, proper accountability, and a few necessary tools, failure could be just around the corner. Failure is seeking out every pastor, every leader, and every voice for God in our society. Where better for evil to attack pastors than with sexual integrity. We live in a world where stimulation confronts us from every angle. The messages and images in the media elevate the probability of failure.

The stories Ray shares in this book help both the fallen and the susceptible to fall. There are only two categories: Those who have fallen and those who are targeted to fall. Through Ray's work, all pastors can find the support and truth necessary to succeed as God's messengers and servants. I don't think there has ever been a more critical time for a book on this topic than now.

Pastors fall from the graces of their families, friends, church congregation, and fellow pastors in one swoop. The pastor who the day before the fall was accepted and admired experiences another depth of loneliness and abandonment; from the top to the bottom almost immediately. The guilt and shame of the sin catapults the pastor into isolation and despair.

Life can literally change in a flash, a moment, in one bad decision. I received a late night phone call from Bob and I knew something had gone desperately wrong. He confessed his struggle, his addiction, and ultimately his crime. Bob's life was about to change forever. Bob moved from an admirable pastor in the community to what many called a despicable human being. When the world says you have lost all value where do we turn? How do we climb out of the hole we have dug and experience a new level of health?

Ray points us back to the reality of a loving God who lifts us past our sin and invites us to a new way of living. All people experience heartbreak and all people experience disappointment, but not all people grasp the newness and redemption that comes from Christ. You may find yourself believing that God's grace covers the sins of those in your church that have fallen, but not me. God has trusted me and I have failed Him. At XXXchurch. com we believe that no person, no pastor, no city leader, no sports star, no celebrity, and no political figure is outside of the grasp of God's grace. I believe this message is the foundation of Ray's work. God has a deep desire to seek out those who are hurting and extend grace.

You will learn from the stories he shares and the journey of others. Many smart people (way smarter than me) have shared their knowledge, their experiences, and their expertise to make this book a manual for pastors. You will read many things in this book that are never taught in bible colleges and seminaries across the country. Many have neglected to tackle the issue of sexual integrity in pastoral education. This may be the number one topic to address in equipping pastors, and yet few classes are honest to prospective pastors about the threat. Pornography and sexual integrity is the number one threat to pastors today.

I encourage you to take this threat to your ministry and life seriously. Identify the dangers and disciplines necessary to survive before it is too late. Learn from those who have gone before – those who have fallen and survived and those who have denied the lure of sexual sin.

Thanks to the words of Ray Carroll we are reminded that there is hope, there is renewal, and there is grace. I am cheering for you in this battle for your life. For some of you this is a new beginning. I pray you will take the words in this book seriously and pass them on to others who are heading down a destructive path. Allow God's grace to catapult you into an entirely new way of living!

Jake Larson

XXXchurch.com

Section One

The Crisis At Hand

Pastors across the country are burning out at an alarming rate. According to one study, 1,500 pastors a month are leaving due to burnout, conflict or moral failure. The eventual path of some of these pastors leads them to moral failure. The landscape is deep with pastors who have fallen and are either seeking help or are still searching for a helping hand. The literature to date has been almost entirely how to help the church heal after a pastor has fallen. Very few books exist to help a fallen minister pick up the pieces and put his life back together. Yet reconciliation is only truly possible when both are restored. The lingering effects of resentment always cripple those who never seek reconciliation and restoration.

Not many in the church have room in their heart for compassion for the fallen minister. His sin is considered enormous. He leaves hurt people in his wake, harms his family and wife, and the expectations of the church are destroyed. However, the pain of the fallen pastor starts long before he even begins to consider his indiscretion as a reasonable solution. The pain after the fall is just as significant as the guilt, shame and realization piling up upon his heart.

This book exists primarily for three reasons. First, it is for those who have fallen from grace, are trying to make sense of life and are seeking restoration and peace. The journey towards restoration is a long process in today's climate, but it is possible. Second, it exists to reach out to those who have been affected by the fallen pastor's choices. This book does not exist to make excuses or to justify any pastor's indiscretion. When we understand the depth of the problem, and the root issues behind it, we can begin to engage compassion and healing for the wounds that exist. And finally, it exists to provide a helpful guide to prevent failure, and to aid those who would take up the call to walk by a fallen pastor in his most desperate hour. When I fell from the ministry, such a resource as this was not available and would have been foundational to my healing.

I want this book to help fallen pastors to understand the process after their fall, know they are not alone and seek the help they need. There are many out there who believe they are alone and useless. They are not. They are men who have been called by Christ to a task and still have a redemptive purpose. I also want this book to be a path for ministers to avoid moral failure in ministry. Hopefully by seeing the signs within their church and in their own life, they can humble themselves instead of saying, "that will never happen to me." Finally, I pray that churches, especially their leaders, will read this and understand that pastors are tremendously human – before and after a fall. Churches need to understand how brittle and in need of love their pastor is. After a fall, a fallen pastor is still a man who should be communicated with; whether by the church he harmed or by a new church that is equipped to reach out to help heal him. The fallen pastor is still a man of worth to God.

Dr. Hershael York, professor at The Southern Baptist Theological Seminary used this analogy:

> "It's like a diamond being cut and polished. I saw this happen once in Tel Aviv. I asked the man cutting the diamond, 'What happens if you make a misktake? What happens if you cut too deep?' The cutter said, 'Well, then I have to go and cut every other side exactly like that to match.' So I said, 'If you miscut you've diminished the value of it.' He said, 'Absolutely.' I think of it like that. A man who has fallen, there's no question he's diminished something. He's still a diamond and of great worth, but he's not what he could have been had he not fallen."[1]

On the one hand, it seems to be that the church holds the pastor in a sort of awe where he is placed upon a pedestal. There should be high expectations for a minister. Scripture places high moral and spiritual expectations upon leaders within the church. Church members should show respect for all spiritual leaders within the church who are called. However, the line is crossed when unrealistic high expectations are placed upon him and he is seen as the spiritual leader of his community but he is seen as more than a sinner, saved by grace. He is approached for counseling, spiritual advice, financial advice, marital issues and sought out in times of crisis. Week after week, he stands in a place of authority with God's Word in hand, doling out the truth. How can such a man, girded with such truth, fall?

Although this book focuses on stories of adultery, the word can easily be replaced with embezzlement, abuse, or anything that could be considered a serious breach of character. The point is not to justify adultery but to show the common patterns that can contribute to virtually the same outcome.

Listening To Why

My fall occurred in 2009 at the end of an eight-year tenure at a Southern Baptist Church with a membership of around 80. After my fall, I began to ask many questions about the situation I had created for myself. At the time I felt alone in the world with few friends I could turn to. I wondered if the feelings of personal anger, depression, despair and desire for reconciliation were unique to me. I wondered if there were other broken pastors who shared a similar story or if there were ministries dedicated to helping people like me.

I began to anonymously blog about my experience, hoping to chase some of the "demons" out of my head and perhaps find those who had common experiences. Within weeks, I found there were many fallen ministers who shared a common bond with me. A year later, I was receiving emails and phone calls from ministers who were about to commit adultery and those who had already fallen. I was incapable of solving their problems, but I could share my experience with them, pray with them, sit with them and tell them the truth of what I knew. A few months later I was approached to write this book and answer an important question.

We know pastors fall, but what circumstances contribute to that fall? These are ministers who have dedicated their lives to the gospel and most often have been tried and proven to be strong. How can a man with such strength fall so easily? Moreover, how can it be prevented? The danger for a fallen pastor to write a book such as this is that I might appear to be justifying my sin. That is the furthest thing from the truth. I will quote other fallen pastors, counselors, church leaders and experts in my desire to help all those affected by a minister's moral failure.

It still may seem strange to write a book and not have a motive other than self-justification. I do hope to help fallen pastors make sense of what they have been through so they can be restored. The fallen pastor's story is not often told, and quite frankly, is not one many care to hear. But it is instructive not just for fallen ministers but for church leaders, parishioners and those who desire to help.

Two weeks after my fall from ministry, I ran into a former church member in public. My emotions were still raw and I was still swimming in a sea of my hurt and sin. She asked me, "Why, Brother Ray? Why did you do it?" Her question was sincere. I had hurt her and she was searching for answers of her own, but I had no answers to give. I suppose if I had been honest at that raw, emotional moment, I could have said, "I was confused with my life because of the death of my parents, I'm a filthy sinner, I sought comfort in the arms of someone who gave me that comfort and honestly, I'm still trying to figure it out." Did I say that? No. All I could muster that day at K-Mart was, "I don't know." No answer would have soothed her heart or given her peace while she went through the grieving process and her disappointment over what I had done. Even if I had given that answer, much of it would have sounded like justification and excuses to her.

I have imagined that same conversation taking place today. I've had two years to digest the pain, the circumstances, the relationships, the church issues, my own sin and all the events that led up to the moment of my adultery. Now, with a different view on the matter, if she approached me, my answer would be completely different. I would say, "You know, I'm sorry about what I did and how it affected your life. I can never take it back. I've learned to own up to my sin since that day I saw you two years ago. I have no excuse for the sin I committed, it was all mine. I've learned since then that God has been more gracious to me than I have ever deserved or could possibly imagine. The man I was before I fell is not the same man I am now and I am thankful for that. He took my mess and made it into his message. Unfortunately through a trying set of circumstances in life, church and family, I found myself in a place where I was searching. I'm happy to say now that God worked all things together for His good and I am extremely blessed with my life, my wife and my children."

When I think back to that meeting with that woman, answering "why" is important. When we begin to answer why, we can begin to process what happened in the event so we can reach a space of reconciliation. If the Gospel means anything, it is to seek out those who are brokenhearted and restore. To answer why is to engage that sense of restoration. But answering why also requires seeing the human being that exists inside the idol that is commonly called a pastor. The role is fraught with an almost insurmountable expectation to be perfect, and no human being, with one exception, has been perfect.

The answer to this question in a larger sense required listening to the stories of other men who have fallen. In the following chapters, some of these men have willingly shared the story of their own fall. Within these stories one will find many common threads that lead a pastor to become broken. I will lead these stories with my own fall. Each of the stories is very real, but I have changed the names to protect these men as well as the churches in which they fell. Details and locations have been altered for their sake, but their basic stories have been saved to relate the tragedy of their fall. Each chapter also includes discussion questions for small groups or classes who wish to examine the issues further.

Some of the stories presented do not resolve with the pastor and his wife reconciling. In some cases, the fallen pastor and his wife divorce, his life takes a turn for the worse and he does not find repentance or restoration until sometime later. These stories are not presented as a model for pastors to follow in the event of a crisis. They are simply the record of occurrences in the midst of our culture. They are a reflection of a larger problem and each story is unique yet they all have a common thread.

After unfolding these stories, a closer examination will be made of the common experiences before and after these falls as well as the social situations within the churches. The question that is asked most often, "Why do pastors fall?" will be addressed. Finally, recovery and prevention will be examined. It is often said that Christians "shoot their wounded." Many fallen pastors find themselves isolated after a fall but are in desperate need of forgiveness and redemption. Can a fall be prevented? If it can, what needs to change in the heart of the church and the minister?

Chapter 1

How Can I Fall?

The modern church is hemorrhaging pastors at an alarming rate. Pastors are leaving and staying away from the ministry. Many of these men claim to be burned out and some cite church conflict as a reason for their departure. Some of them are caught in adultery and are forced to resign. The men who break the seventh commandment have sinned and are cast out quickly. Yet what if the circumstances behind their sin are similar to the men who left due to conflict or burnout? What if they were just as relieved to leave the ministry as the other pastors? It is a symptom of a larger problem within the church culture when a pastor abandons his call through adultery as an escape from the circumstances that steadily grew around him.

It is a story that repeats itself hundreds of times a month. It is occurring as you read these words, probably in a church somewhere near you. A pastor is sitting at home, contemplating adultery. His mind is racing as he fears the present, wonders about the future and is terrified of being discovered. He has given his life to his church, week after week, listening to problems within the congregation, baptizing the converts, visiting the elderly, yet he now finds himself trapped.

His marriage has been suffering for years from poor communication and he has now found someone who would listen. The communication he once enjoyed with his wife has dropped off severely in the past few years due to his increased level of commitment to the ministry. While the church sees a man devoted to God, his wife sees a man who has isolated himself from the world. Their intimacy has suffered and they have grown apart while keeping up the façade of the perfect ministry couple.

On one hand, he has a church that has placed overly zealous expectations upon him for visitation, winning souls, preaching, and maintaining attendance. He has probably agreed to those expectations and drives himself harder than any church member could. The appreciation and adoration that his wife once gave him has now been replaced with the admiration of the church. He chases after the ministry accolades harder and harder each week to fill the void. The gap has widened further and further between him and his wife, even to the point where he is miserable in his marriage. To leave his marriage would mean the end of his ministry. His whole life has been poured into the service of the church, yet being a divorced pastor just doesn't work in ministry circles.

He has few friends, if any, he is able to confide in within the church, and he is frightened to share his ministry struggles with his pastor friends. A pastor is supposed to be a beacon of light and strength, and signs of weakness are likely not tolerated, or even discussed. In a few cases, his friends might even understand his feelings, but are unwilling to admit they have struggles of their own for fear of being outcast. The pastor might even perceive that his friends wouldn't understand the struggle he is undergoing, so he crawls deeper into the recesses of his fears and doubts. This disconnection from community leads to a profound level of loneliness and isolation.

To fill the void of loneliness, he found for comfort from another woman close to him within the church or on his staff. It likely started as a harmless friendship. She understood him and his struggles and they just "clicked." He knew he should stay away from her, he knew it was sinful, but he craved her attention and acceptance. He was overjoyed when he finally found someone who was able to share his pain and listen to him. He saw her as a Godsend and an answer to prayer. She had similar spiritual and life problems. At first, they just enjoyed talking, baring their souls to one another. She filled the void in his life of spiritual and emotional connectedness to another person. The relationship slowly accelerated into an emotional gray area as they emailed, texted and looked forward to seeing one another at church. Neither of them would admit to the other that they knew things were serious, and both would deny it if anyone asked.

They exchanged meaningful but quick touches that sent chills down the other's spine. All of it was seemingly harmless until they had "the talk." It was spurred on by the one who was willing to admit the relationship was more than just friendship. Ultimately, they were faced with a question that had to be answered. It was one rife with moral, spiritual and life consequences - where would they go from here?

The conversation led to a critical crossroads. He could walk away from the relationship and back to the loneliness that drove him to her in the first place. Or he could leave it all behind and consummate the emotional relationship, with hope of a better future. He had counted the cost of losing his family, abandoning his ministry and letting people down – or he believes he has. He lives in the present, knowing that he wants to be happy and understood. He wants to be free of the restraints of expectations. He wants to be free of a relationship in which he has no communication or comfort. Or maybe he simply wants to be free of a church that isn't functioning or listening to him anymore.

Some will think he's entering into a "cheap" relationship. Maybe he is. Maybe he really loves this woman. Maybe he's deceived himself. Maybe it's all three. He does know the sin involved, but he's justified it every step of the way. Every time conviction comes to his mind, he pushes it down again, far below his hazed line of morality. "I can keep it under control. This is God's plan for my life."

But then something likely happens, like a fight with his wife, or a berating from a demanding church member, that seems to call everything into question about his life. The "other women" is the only one who seems to understand his fears and his pain. And just like that he falls into a physical relationship with a woman whom he believes now understands him better than he's ever been understood. Or he might just abandon himself to whim, jumping in but unsure of its real meaning and finding no hope in the alternative.

During the encounter, he has a mix of elation and guilt, knowing he has crossed his own personal Rubicon. After the encounter, he will either be more certain that his decision was correct, or he will regret it and do whatever he can to cover up his mistake.

Ultimately, his sin will find him out. After his sin is discovered, there are a myriad of reactions to this betrayal. Church leadership, ill equipped to deal with such a situation, will react harshly and bitterly. In their hurt, they demand his resignation in order to separate him as quickly as possible from the congregation. The membership goes through an array of individual responses. Most members are shocked and angry and few are able to grant forgiveness or show compassion in a relatively short amount of time. Most local pastors will separate themselves, treating him like a modern day leper, but a few will reach out in sincerity.

The fallen pastor is now truly isolated. If his wife decides to stand by his side, they now find themselves alone. If she leaves him or if he gives up on their marriage, he is alone. No one will feel sorry for him because he has been trapped in his own tangled web of deceit and lies. No sympathy will come, only harsh words and compounding gossip. He has no ministry career anymore and the likelihood of turning further away from God at this point in his life is very high.

Just a few years ago, he probably thought he had life under control. His church looked to him for support and advice, his family was all under one roof, he was receiving the love and attention he needed, and he had respect. Now, because of his sin, his own decisions, he has been cast aside. He has become a statistic and a reprobate. In the coming weeks, he will be faced with the reality of divorce, unemployment, unforgiveness and being the most hated man in his community. Suicide may cross his mind as he lives alone for the first time since he got married. He will at first lash out at those in the church, but as the night watch comes, he will turn his anger toward himself. This is the new life of the fallen pastor.

A Pastoral Idol

The path from pastor to idol has been slowly entrenched into church culture for some time. It happens so subtly that many do not realize it is happening. After a fall occurs, most do not even realize that the culture had a large role to play. The process takes time, but is taking place in churches all across the country. These stories don't just happen. They happen within a very common culture. Many church cultures include a common and dangerous idolization of the pastor, which leads to unrealistic expectations and eventually isolation.

Pastors often come into their role from a seminary background where they have been trained to be the experts in the things of God. Even without seminary, pastors carry with them a special calling upon their lives to lead and shepherd, which they take very seriously. They see before them unlimited opportunities as their hearts are filled with passion for what they can accomplish.

The pastor is supposed to be the shining example and beacon of light to the community. His entry into the church is often welcomed with great praise and he may be seen as the way to growth and revival. Before his entry into the ministry, the pastor was not a public speaker and did not command the attention of many. Now, he finds himself speaking the words of God before a congregation each Sunday who look to him for advice and help. This swing from lowliness to greatness can be cause for high expectations in himself and from others. He works long hours to perform acts of service at the expense of his marriage and family. The return for performing these actions is a thriving church which heaps praise upon him, placing him upon a pedestal.

Most churches have a reverent awe concerning their pastor. They attach a tag to him: Reverend or Brother. They train their children to address him by that name. Even if a church member has a strong dislike for the pastor, they often will still hold reverence for his office if they don't respect the man behind the pulpit. Certain attributes about a minister increase both respect and expectations from churches, it would seem: Seminary training, number of children, years in ministry and length of stay at his church and age. The church may look upon the pastor's attributes and God given gifts as a reason to brag upon him or expect more from him. Admiration of him is normal and biblical, but it can move to something more extreme. He is the center of the church community and the repository of knowledge about God.

This deep admiration is great for the ego but harmful to the soul. Unless this admiration is approached with humility and a Christ-like attitude, pastors will find themselves the object of something that is akin to worship. He may even become more to them than a pastor. He becomes an idol, a destructive image that is completely different than the meek man he was called to be.

A differentiation needs to be made between normal high expectations and the dangerous idolatry that can occur. Churches should have high expectations for their pastor. Scripture places high expectations upon leaders. Churches should expect that their pastor will not commit adultery. God holds His leaders to a very high standard. It should be shocking when a man of God falls because he was trusted with the care of the people of God and His Word and in that care, he committed great hypocrisy. That expectation is different than the idolatry discussed here. Idolatry that is dangerous in the church culture is when a pastor is pushed into a higher realm of expectation than is physically, emotionally or mentally acceptable. It is when the weight of the work of the church is placed upon him unrealistically. It is when more than should be reasonably expected, even by the bible, is placed upon him. Or, it is when those around him elevate him to a status higher than human, seeing him as infallible or more than human.

When a pastor rises to the place of an idol, a trap is set. It is the first part of a cycle that has been in place for decades and can eventually lead to ministry failure. Those who participate in the broken culture are vastly unaware that it is taking place. The proof of the problem can be seen with the eventual results that plague the church – a landscape littered with fallen and broken ministers.

Many pastors will become idols in their church culture. The problem occurs when they accept this position of idolatry. If a pastor chooses to be viewed greater than he is, he will fall into the trap. When he chooses to take on the mantle that he is strong, bulletproof and invincible, he begins the slide downward. The trap can lead to many things – fatigue, stress, health problems, burnout, church conflict and even sexual sin.

When the pastor agrees to the expectations of the church and places pressure upon himself to become a self-realized idol, he does whatever he can to please his church and he may begin to chase after its approval.

The Mistress

Most people think a fallen pastor has an affair with only a woman. But this wouldn't be true. There is always a mistress that precedes her, one that virtually no one sees. Church of God Counselor Bill Leonard believes that when a pastor places the duty of ministry before his family, difficulties will likely arise, causing the spouse and family to feel neglected:

> "A lot of ministers have what we call the 'mistress', which is the church. They're eating supper, the phone rings and the mistress has called. They're getting ready to take a vacation, something in the church happens and the vacation is cancelled. The mistress has taken precedence over the family."[2]

Bill Leonard used a strong choice of words to describe the pastor's relationship to the church – "mistress." This denotation would suggest that many pastors have already forsaken the priorities in their lives for something else. The culture of the church has taken precedence over their family and become their love. The passion for the culture of the church should be radically distinguished by the love of Christ, which should supersede all. When the pastor begins to chase after his standing within the culture, his family will usually suffer.

The mistress of ministry demands lots of attention. And once he's tasted her bounty and her affections, he will do whatever it takes to please her, to sacrifice for her and to make her great in the eyes of the public. If a decision has to be made between family and the church, the pastor will choose the church. The mistress, the church, is not the same as the true body of Christ. The mistress of ministry is harsh and demanding, it is the overwhelming passion of success that becomes addictive. Within it are the payoffs of appreciation and acceptance.

While he pursues this mistress, he finds little time for his wife and family. According to the Francis Schaeffer Institute of Church Leadership, 77% of pastors reported they did not have a good marriage.[3] Communication issues arise and intimacy becomes a serious problem. Instead of being a safe place for pastoral couples, the ministry culture becomes a destructive place for marriages.

Each Sunday, the minister shares knowledge about God, becoming the spokesman for God. Some may internalize his leadership to an extreme, turning him into a type of golden calf. He becomes a superman. If he does not find a way to downplay this and continue to seek humility before them, he may attract admirers. Men will idolize his teaching and wish to mirror his speaking and appearance. Some women may even become attracted to him. Some might look at him and say, "Why can't my husband be more like him? Why can't he have it all together like him? Why can't he be caring and loving like him?" Having this kind of admiration for the pastor at church can be dangerous for him when he doesn't receive an equal amount at home, leading him further into the trap.

The mistress is magnified when he moves from smaller church to larger church. He may see the move as a conquest, increasing his pride if he is not wary of his relationship with God. The pastor, deep in his heart, may even expect to be idolized or respected by his congregation. He may begin to dress like, look like and act like the ministers in his denomination who have "made it" or respond to positive feedback as if it were a drug. As the years pass, a prideful pastor is able to add accomplishment after accomplishment to his resume, building up his ego while he loses sight of the main reason for ministry.

It is important to state that the pastor is to blame for his part in the process. He accepts this charge from the church, agrees to their high expectations, does not tell them of his weakness and works himself harder and harder the worse things become. This creates in him a sense of isolation from those who could help. The trap looms larger as his relationship with his spouse weakens, his pride enlarges and he never discusses the great expectations that are upon him with his church leadership. Eventually, he begins to break and feel unappreciated or disrespected. He knows he needs rest or support but feels he has nowhere to go. Many solutions cross his mind, but it is here that the new mistress takes form, in the affections of a member of the opposite sex. Before he understands what has happened, the pastor finds himself snared by the trap. Everything he once knew to be sacred is gone.

Of course, the church with the idol culture is shocked when they discover the idol they have built for themselves is nothing more than flesh and blood. The problem with idols is that they are there for us to gaze upon in the perfection we have molded in them. They are a fantasy and do not correlate with reality. Idols have no weaknesses and we can add whatever characteristics we desire. They need perfection to keep them from seeing their own faults. When pastors become idols, failure is not an option. There can be no weakness. Instead of actively pursuing forgiveness or compassion, the church acts like a woman scorned, pushing his memory aside, divorcing him from their fellowship. When the idols of old could not bring rain or heal diseases, they were cast aside. When we see the pastor fall, he is easily cast aside for the next idol that can be appointed pastor.

Unless the culture within the church is willing to be examined and addressed, a new trap is set for the next minister.

Examining The Larger Cultural Landscape

Moral failure occurs all too frequently in churches throughout denominations across the world. According to the following statistics, one in three active pastors admits to having an affair, 70% of pastors deal with depression, seven out of ten report having no close friends. The problem is not just the individuals involved but also the culture that creates the trap in the first place. Behind these sins are real people who have given in to temptation while being broken by a system.

It is easy to look at ministers who have fallen and cast a judgmental eye without trying to understand the path that led to their sin in the first place. Many statistical studies have been done to examine the life of the average pastor. On the outside, the American pastor on Sunday gives the impression of a spiritual giant, unaffected by the common problems of the world. He smiles, he preaches the Word, he shares encouragement, and his happy family looks like a paradigm for the church to follow. However, the numbers tell a different story.

The Focus on the Family Newsletter reported these startling statistics in 1998[4]:

- 80% of pastors and 84% of their spouses are discouraged and dealing with depression
- More than 40% of pastors and 47% of their spouses report they are suffering from burnout, frantic schedules and unrealistic expectations
- Approximately 1,500 pastors leave their assignments each month due to moral failure, spiritual burnout, or contention within their local congregations

The Francis Schaeffer Institute of Church Leadership has twice done studies among evangelical pastors with similar and alarming results. They sampled pastor's conferences with sizes of at least 600:[5]

- 89% of pastors stated they considered leaving the ministry at one time
- 57% said they would leave if they had a better place to go (including secular work)
- 77% said they felt they did not have a good marriage
- 71% stated they were burned out and they battle depression beyond fatigue on a weekly and even a daily basis
- 30% said they had either been in an ongoing affair or a one-time sexual encounter with a parishioner

In an article for the Los Angeles Times, Richard Blackmon relayed the following statistics:[6]

- 30-40% of ministers ultimately drop out of ministry
- 75% go through a period of stress so great, they consider quitting

In an article on pastors and marriage problems, Leadership magazine reported the following troubling statistics:[7]

- 81% of pastors report insufficient time with their spouse
- 64% report communication difficulties
- 46% report sexual problems

The Fuller Institute of Church Growth performed a study in which they reported the following information about pastors:[8]

- 90% work more than 46 hours a week
- 80% believed pastoral ministry affected their families negatively
- 33% believed ministry was a hazard to their ministry
- 75% reported a significant stress related crisis at least once in their ministry
- 50% felt themselves unable to meet the needs of the job
- 90% felt inadequately trained to cope with ministry demands
- 70% say they have a lower self-esteem now compared to when they started in ministry
- 40% reported serious conflict with a parishioner at least once a month
- 37% confessed to having been involved in inappropriate sexual behavior with someone in the church
- 70% do not have someone they consider a close friend

These numbers reveal how serious the problem is and that there has been trouble brewing in the American church for quite some time. Fallen pastors are responsible for their adultery, but unless the problem underlying cultural issues that support the problem is addressed, the cycle is likely to continue.

Chapter 2

A Well-Deserved Perfect Storm

"Do you want to tell me about this affair you're having?" my wife said with storms brewing in her eyes. She had woken up at six in the morning. Anger filled her voice. I already knew what it was about. She was a woman who was never prone to anger.

I quickly woke, searching for the right words that would somehow justify myself. But I knew the lies would do me no good. "What?" was all I could muster. I slowly rose out of the bed, looking for an escape, for a way to talk myself out of the situation. I was hoping for divine intervention, but knew that God was a million miles away from my heart.

"With Allison," she said as she threw down a printed stack of emails on the bed.

For the first time in a confrontation, I was speechless. I looked at her eyes that once reflected love and now all they held was anger. They demanded answers from me that I wasn't willing to give. Tears started welling up in her eyes, but she held them back.

My body and heart began to tense up, desiring to fight back, to blame my problems on her and the stress of my life, but I knew it was futile. It was finally time for the truth. A few weeks before, I had resigned my pastorate and given a month's notice. My wife and I were seeking a separation because of our marriage problems that had been going on for years. We had been able to control them, but due to recent crises, they were now spiraling out of control. The church thought my resignation was because I was stressed out. I knew the truth. It was because I had committed adultery and wanted to be with Allison.

I relented. "What do you want to know?" I asked.

In a lot of ways I was relieved to ask that question. No more lies, no more deceit, no more hiding. At that moment, despite the crushing pain on my soul of being caught and catching a glimpse of the pain I had caused, I also felt tremendous relief. I felt free from church conflict, free from hiding, free from a relationship that had been deteriorating for a long time. I also realized the paradox of the landslide I now found myself in.

I had been dying on the inside for a long time, even before I had met Allison. I had been chasing after an unrealistic view of myself that I could never achieve. I knew others had expectations for me and believed in me and I was tired of pretending to be the "man in the pulpit" on Sunday only to realize that I was a wretch every other day of the week. I had kept the charade up for a long time. Even though that day was horrible, it opened up the realization that I was tired of chasing after my own dreams of unrealistic perfection.

The perfect storm had been brewing for some time, but its fury had yet to be unleashed. I had missed the signs. Church problems, marriage issues and life crises; all of the elements were there and it was a matter of time before its clouds ripped open and the storm began to rage. When it began, I had no appreciation of its power or its longevity, but I was about to discover that I was woefully unprepared.

I typically slept late due to the demands of pastoring a bi-vocational church. I worked a sports medicine job in the afternoon and fulfilled my pastoral duties early in the day. I was a night owl and stayed up very late. Recently, however, I had been staying up late talking to Allison through text or email chat. She was a member of my church whom I had connected to recently and more specifically, fallen in love with. During the rising storm in my life, I had begun to disassociate from everything I had known because I had felt my faith, my marriage, family and church drifting away from me. Allison was the only one who reached out to me in my pleas for help. Over time, we came together and found love like we had never known.

One night, I left my email open before I went to bed. My wife had been distressed because of our marriage problems and had woken up early. She found my open email and discovered some very damning evidence that exposed the affair. The betrayal she felt must have been devastating as she viewed it. As I lay in bed getting my last good night's sleep, she printed them out and opened the bedroom door and confronted me with my adultery.

For the next hour, she asked rapid-fire questions that I barely heard. I knew better than to give details because they would fuel her anger further. Our kids were still asleep and my heart and mind kept going to them, knowing I had betrayed them as well. I could only imagine the brutal fallout that would ensue. I had been the one to comfort her when she had been hurt over the years. Now, I was the one causing her the most pain and there was nothing I could do about it. She was angry, mad, and hurt. And she had every right to be.

"How could you do that with my best friend? Why couldn't it have been someone I didn't know? Now I've lost a husband and a best friend!" Her final question to me was the one that would do me in for good, "Do you love her?" Her teary eyes awaited a response that did not hesitate coming out of my mouth.

"Yes, I do." I watched her heart break for good with that answer. It whipped the storm into a rage as she was lost to me forever, her eyes deepening with hurt, turning into the well-deserved perfect storm.

From there, she insisted we go talk to the church leadership and that I confess my sin. I refused for prideful reasons. I wanted her to help me conceal my sin until my notice was up. It was a selfishly stupid request, but she was insistent. Within the hour, I was confessing my sin to one of the deacons and I was giving my second resignation. I was told to never return to the church and to have an official letter drafted for the next business meeting. I was asked by my wife to leave the parsonage immediately.

We drove back home where my kids were waiting. They had no idea what was going on, and I had no idea what to say to them. I had been the one to have to tell them of their grandparent's death and now I was about to level this news on them. Their father wouldn't be living with them anymore – and it was my fault. It was because of my sin. I gathered them on the couch in the living room.

"Girls, Daddy has to leave for a while. I've done something terrible," I said, eyes already filling with tears.

Abigail and Katie, nine and six, looked at me curiously, "What did you do?"

"Daddy broke a commandment," I said. "The seventh one." They knew their commandments through a finger numbering technique. Both of them started counting on their fingers trying to do the math.

Simultaneously, they said with wide eyes, "Adultery?" They knew, but didn't really know what it meant, but they were sure it was serious.

"That's right. And I don't expect you to forgive me today, but someday I will need you to and,"

Abigail interrupted me and said, "Of course we forgive you, you're our daddy!" They hugged me at the same time. My little girls will never know what that moment meant to me as I sat on the couch and cried with them, holding them as tightly as I could. I felt like the worst human being in the world and a failure as a father, but their unconditional love and acceptance for me was a better sermon than I had preached in my entire life. It was a moment I would cherish deeply, as it would be the only forgiveness I would receive for quite some time.

I quickly packed up what clothes I could into a black, plastic trash bag and drove to an empty rental house in the next county. As I drove, I recalled part of the conversation I had earlier with my wife. She had reminded me that before we were married she had told me if I ever cheated on her, she would never reconcile with me. She couldn't believe I would betray her with her best friend. Her words rang true and reconciliation would never come.

Communication Breakdowns

In a blog I started a year after my fall, I reflected on the events that led to my choice to have an affair:

"I sinned and have no one to blame but myself. When my wife discovered that I had cheated, I gave her no excuse. I suppose I could've told her that our relationship had been faltering for years, that our intimacy had been suffering, that the personal tragedies surrounding us had caused me depression, or that church life had been insufferable and that she had never really talked to me about them. But I didn't. The blame for my actions lay squarely on my shoulders. However, the events that led up to my sin did have a profound impact upon me."

To really understand why, it is important to acknowledge that circumstances do play a part in any pastor's failure. Ultimately, he cannot blame circumstance. We stand alone in our sin. But we all follow a path to the decisions we make. My life was no different.

My wife did not marry a pastor. I received my call to ministry while working on my master's degree to further my career in sports medicine. After entering the ministry, our communication issues were obvious. For some reason, my wife and I had always had difficulty communicating about the ministry and sharing about the problems I had in church. Instead of being able to lean on my wife for support, I leaned on my mother for the help and encouragement I needed. Mom became my confidant, my sole sounding board for ministry problems. Mom moved to the area where I pastored after she and my father divorced.

Being a bi-vocational pastor offered a new set of difficulties. I was required to perform a full time role in a part time space. It included preaching, visiting, growing the church, managing conflict, teaching and balancing all of these tasks at once. While all that was occurring, I felt like a hero to many. On Sundays, I felt like a different man. I was being praised for results and the good things that were happening. During the week, I knew my weaknesses and shortcomings. The expectations that some had for me had placed me higher than I ever should have been. In my mind, there was a battle raging. At times, I was the phenomenal pastor who was able to do all things for all people. At others, I felt weak and unworthy of my job.

To be fair, I placed higher expectations upon myself than the church ever could. But there were very high expectations placed upon me through passing comments, emails, suggestions and concerned members. The burden was heavy and I took it very seriously. Like most ministers, I often felt inferior and unappreciated as a pastor. For every compliment there were six complaints. I would get selfishly angry year after year when Pastor Appreciation Sunday would roll around and no formal recognition would occur. "A card, or a gift certificate, something!" I would think.

I sought support and encouragement at home, but conversation about things at church was lacking. I just figured being woefully underappreciated was part of the job. The problem was not isolated. Many of my pastor friends shared that they hardly ever heard positive feedback either. One friend of mine would continue to tell me, "Suck it up, Ray. You're not in the ministry to get a pat on the back. They either like you or they don't. You're here to work for Jesus." That didn't help much, especially when I had a constant need for affirmation.

Two years after my parents divorced, my father died in an accident. He and I had experienced an adversarial relationship since my teenage years, which caused even more stress. After his death, I began to regret reaching out to him and sought counseling. After he died I carried around a lot of unresolved anger about our relationship. During that time, my preaching reflected much of this unnecessary anger. I needed Mom more than ever.

After Dad's death, the church had several crises occur which almost broke me. People were arguing over things I felt were inconsequential to the Kingdom of God, but they seemed very important to some in the church. Many times I would go home and weep, other times my anger got the better of me and I became confrontational. These problems in church placed even higher stress on me and several times I sent out resumes to other churches. I'd go home and complain, but realized that my wife didn't want to hear about it much of the time. Instead, I'd go see Mom, who was there to listen and support me. If someone in the church was angry with me or gossiping, I would immediately call her or go see her. Her wise words always calmed me down.

A year and a half after my father's death, my family packed up for the Christmas holiday to go see my wife's family who lived two hours away. After spending a night there, I woke up the next morning with an awful feeling. I called Mom repeatedly and couldn't get an answer. She was always obsessive compulsive about answering her phone, but for some reason wasn't answering. Finally, a church member called and told me that Mom had been badly injured in a car accident. On our way home, we would learn that she had died on the way to the hospital. It was the day before Christmas Eve. The church was overwhelmingly supportive to me and gave me space to grieve, knowing I was suffering immensely.

> *Within my grief, I found myself questioning the "why" of life. They were the questions pastors hear all the time but aren't supposed to ask themselves: "Why did this happen? Why did God allow it?" I had been in a position of ministry for almost ten years, helping people grieve and giving good answers to them for a long time. Those answers seemed to work. But not now. Not for me. It's difficult to minister to a minister because we think we know it all. We know all the pat answers to give to people, but we just don't know how to listen. I went to a Christian counselor I knew and struggled with the answers as I spoke to her. It helped a little as did some medication. But nothing helped the deep, awful hurt that I experienced every day. I dug deeper into my work and buried my feelings as far as I could.*

Mom had become my strongest and only ally in life. She had been my greatest prayer warrior from the day I was born. She had been my sounding board and resting place. I had a couple of pastor friends, but they were hundreds of miles away. I suddenly realized terribly I had become isolated with no one to confide in. Mom had always been the one I had called when there was good news or bad news to share and now she was gone. Pastors often find it hard to make close friends. I reflected on this on my blog after my fall:

> *"When you're pastoring, you love the people you pastor. You shepherd them, preach to them, do their weddings,*

visit them when they're sick, pray over them, witness to them, teach them . . . but there's something that you don't get to really do. You don't get to be their best friend. Even in seminary, they tell you not to become best friends with any of your church members. It's not a good idea. Church members, I think feel it too. They don't typically befriend the pastor in a close manner. They treat him well, usually, but they don't approach him to be best buddies. I don't know exactly why that instinct exists, exactly. Maybe a lot of pastors are seen to be too 'separate' from the congregation. Maybe it's because the pastor is the 'hired hand,' and you don't get too close because that guy might not be around very long."

After Mom died, I struggled to see any reason to continue in the ministry. Many nights, I just wanted to die. After losing both parents to separate accidents, life suddenly seemed random in contrast to a God whom I once believed was so detailed in His plan. Over time and with help, I remembered again that God was a God of comfort, despite my affliction. Even though He was sovereign, I had trouble understanding my circumstance. I was in a very dark place.

The perfect storm had parked itself right outside my home without me even realizing it. As a pastor, I believed I was strong enough to handle anything that came my way. I thought I could weather any problem, any crisis or conflict within the church, in my life or marriage without any outside help. That belief was falsely bolstered by my faith in my seminary education and my years of experience. What I failed to realize was that I had no support system. My church was still enduring serious conflict and it was placing great stress upon me.

I was grieving the death of both of my parents and my marriage was suffering. I had not sought help for any of it. I didn't know I was weak. In fact, I thought I was strong. Several church members suggested I take time off, but I chose not to. I buried myself in my work, hoping to ease into a rhythm again. I hoped it would comfort me. I was looking for any kind of comfort

I could find. I wasn't looking for comfort outside my marriage, but in the depths of my pain, my heart needed affirmation, comfort and warmth.

The Other Woman

Allison had been a member of the church for several years. She had been through some difficult times of her own. For the time I had known her, I had always admired her strength. I remember the first time I met her and noticed her beauty. Her smile was amazing and she was one of the few people in the church who could tell when I was actually telling a sarcastic joke during one of my sermons. She was outgoing, easy to talk to and eager to help in the church even though she was a full-time mother.

There had been moments where she had crossed my mind and I had wondered what it would have been like to be with her. However, they had been fleeting thoughts. She had troubles of her own and was going through a divorce. She and my mother had become close friends and her death had been painful for her as well. She showed up to the parsonage the day after Mom died and I answered the door. For some reason, we didn't say a word, but just embraced. No one else was there on the doorstep but us and we found strength and comfort from one another. It wasn't a sexual moment, but we connected that day. It would be seven months before we ever seriously began talking or had a conversation, but at that moment, we began to bond to one another. What I had needed and wanted during those days was the comfort of my wife, but instead it was Allison who would give it to me at that moment.

I didn't really think seriously about Allison again until a few months later. I was still reeling from the death of my mother and I was growing tired of the ministry. In the past few years, I had tried on more than one occasion to leave my church and find another, but to no avail. Allison and my wife were best friends and she came around the house fairly often. On one of those occasions, we started talking about some inane topic. She had to leave, but asked me if I texted. I told her I did and gave her my number. We began having conversations and found we had a lot in common. Allison and I had "clicked." We had similar interests, passions and just started talking and really communicating.

It's easy to wonder why I didn't recognize what was happening. And rightfully so, But I hadn't been able to freely open up to anyone like that in a very long time. I had been isolated from people for so long that I had forgotten what it was like to have someone to talk to my own age. With the pain and grief I was still enduring, it was good to have someone who was just interested in me for me.

Each time we texted, the conversation seemed to accelerate. We began to flirt and drop "hints" of attraction toward one another. When we saw each other at church, we would hug and linger with our touch. It was obvious we had deep, mutual attraction for one another. Our conversations became more and more serious as we talked about her divorce and I told her about my grief and how miserable I was in the ministry. One week, I found myself away from work and home and we set up a time to meet. I was nervous, numb and not sure what to expect.

When we got together, I knew what the stakes were. We both did. We had already crossed the emotional barrier. I loved Allison and saw a future with her as more promising than the one I had. I no longer wanted to answer to people, deal with stress or the problems that my anxieties over these issues created. Allison also gave me a rest from the pain I felt and from the grief I endured. Being with her gave me an escape from this life and promised me hope. The only thing that stayed my conscience was my children, but I thought that I could cross that bridge when that moment came. All I knew was that I had a litany of problems and Allison was my cure. That day when we met, we crossed the physical threshold, but did not have sexual intercourse. Even so, I knew there was no going back. I also knew that I did not want to go back to my marriage or the ministry.

Something else came with our encounter – guilt. I knew I had done something I couldn't take back, and I knew I couldn't tell anyone for fear of losing my job. But I also knew talking to Allison again would soothe the guilt. My prideful soul drank all of the relief in that our relationship gave. The past two years had been awful, but the moments I spent with Allison took me away from the pain. Allison had done something for me that no one else had. She comforted me. I needed to feel good and to feel close to someone, even if it meant that I was willfully sinning in the face of God.

I picked her up from work one night and laid everything on the line for her. We still had not consummated our relationship, but I wanted her to know how I felt. I told her, "I love you and I'm willing to give up everything for you. My ministry, my family, my life as I know it. I want to be with you forever." She was speechless. For her, she never believed that I could leave what I had. Even my words were hard to fathom but she held onto them that night.

My wife knew there were serious problems. There had been problems for many years. Instead of being honest with her about my relationship with Allison, I made an appointment to see a specialist. We visited a Christian counselor for marital advice, even though I went with less than noble intentions. Interestingly, at the end of the "Christian counseling" session, we were advised to separate. My wife was devastated. We began to discuss the issue. I knew that above all else, I needed to resign my job as pastor with my emotions pulled toward Allison. My wife and agreed to separate given the poor state of our marriage.

Allison and I set up a time to meet in a nearby town to consummate our relationship. As I waited for her, I thought about the things I would be losing. I knew my marriage and ministry would both be over. They were thoughts that had been with me for the previous weeks, but were now weighing upon me. At that moment, I was ready to leave those two things behind which seemed so broken and so irreparable. The ministry had broken me and offered me no future of hope and my marriage had been suffering for years. I was ready to start something new, even though I knew it was wrong. Allison and I were both nervous, but we went through with it, finding in those few hours the comfort we had been seeking for years.

That Sunday I resigned after I spoke with the deacons. I told them I was burned out, which I was, and that I needed to get away. I did not tell them that my wife and I were seeking a separation or about my relationship with Allison. I gave them a five-week notice. The deacons begged me to stay, but I knew I couldn't. My wife, still unaware of my infidelity, didn't beg me to stay. She told me to move on and separate, calling my bluff. But the truth was, I wanted a different life.

It was my plan to keep my head above water, slide out the back door and hope to have some sort of relationship in the long run with Allison after the dust settled. We were meeting as often as we could. Those few weeks when we were together were like a dizzying whirlwind. I knew I was in the midst of great sin. I knew I was justifying myself. I was lying to my church, my family and committing adultery, but I knew I loved her and wanted to spend the rest of my life with her. The serenity I found with her in the moments we spent together gave me escape from the pain of expectations, grief and isolation. In the time we were apart, my guilt cornered me again, along with the pain and inferiority that had been my partner in the ministry for half a decade.

We had more than one conversation about what we were doing. We knew we were sinning greatly. We knew we were breaking multiple commandments. We knew we were doing it right in front of God's face. All we knew was that we loved each other and wanted to be together. Strangely, I was coming to the point where I hoped I would be discovered. I wanted out of the constraints of the ministry and into a relationship with Allison. The pain upon my conscience was terrible. The weight was becoming hard to bear and Allison and I wanted to be together.

Ironically, I used to be the judgmental pastor upon other people's sin and now I was the hypocrite. I had found the love I needed and was fully pursuing it. In my mind, I knew God's law and ignored it. My mind was swirling with a thousand competing thoughts and the love I had found had trumped all of the tinier voices. I was two different men. I was the pastor who stepped into the pulpit each week, trumpeting the truth of God, calling upon people to be saved. Then, when I walked out of the doors, I was a man seeking comfort and escape from that role.

The Dividing Line

The day my sin was discovered will forever be a dividing line in my life. Before that day, I was a prideful, judgmental man. After that day, the transformation to a broken man began and my heart would be forever changed. The weeks and months after the fall were terrible. There would be no reconciliation between my wife and me. The day she confronted me, I had unleashed emotions in her I had never before seen. I remember having to tell one of the church leaders about my sin. It was a time of great disappointment for him and I recorded the conversation on my blog:

On the way over, I thought about whether he knew it was coming or not. Surely, he had seen Allison and I exchange glances in church. Surely I had betrayed my feelings for her and he had seen it and this wouldn't be a surprise to him. We pulled into his driveway and he was outside with a smile on his face that would soon be wiped away. My heart sank as I walked up to him and he reached out to shake my hand. He knew something was wrong right away. His weathered face frowned immediately, "What's wrong, preacher?"

My heart was in my throat and I was ashamed of myself, as well I should have been. "I have something horrible to tell you." I couldn't even look at my wife.

"What is it?" he asked, his eyes darting back and forth between me and my wife.

"I cheated on my wife," I said looking him in the eyes as I watched pain come over his face, then his mouth drop open.

He staggered backward. "Wha..? You did what? How could you?" He took a moment to gather himself, steadied himself and I saw the anger build. "Why, I oughta pick that stick up over there and beat the fire out of you!"

He probably would have too, if my wife hadn't been standing there. And I would've stood there and taken it. At that moment, I knew I deserved it. I felt awful. Lower than ever in my life. Lower than when I had lost my mother just a few months before. He had been like a father to me. In many ways, better to me than my own father. And if he felt like beating the crap out of me would've made him feel better, I would've let him. It might have made me feel better. Because right then, I deserved a good butt kicking. Over the next fifteen minutes, I got a good lecture. I don't remember it verbatim. But it included things like, "We trusted you, we loved you, she loved you, how could you do this to her, how could you do this to your children, what were you thinking?" After fifteen minutes, I would have rather he just beat me with that stick.

I left the parsonage and my church for the last time after that conversation. I drove to a rental house I had been planning on moving into after my resignation was complete, and on the way called my friend Mike, telling him I was moving in a little early. He didn't have a problem with it because he knew a little about my marriage problems. It was about six in the evening when I arrived. I only had one piece of furniture there - a sofa Mike had donated to me that didn't have any legs on it. The place was in desperate need of a cleaning. All I had was my laptop and a garbage bag full of clothes I had managed to muster up from the parsonage.

It was quiet. No children making happy noises. No phone ringing with church members needing names put on the prayer list. No television with kids shows playing. Silence. I hated silence. But now I had all I could handle. I wanted to call a friend, someone I knew and just talk. To tell them what happened. But how could I? I was ashamed. I was horrified at what I had done to the church I had pastored for eight years. I lay on the couch with a pillow, turned out the lights, and lay there. Thinking of what would happen in the next few days and the wrath I deserved from my wife and from the church. I wondered what the fallout would be. I knew there was no way to prepare myself for the coming storm. There was nothing but deafening silence in the house, but the noise in my mind was loud. More than once, selfish, suicidal thoughts crept into my mind. And I felt at that moment, most of all, that God wouldn't listen to me either.

The following week, my wife told me she had filed for divorce. I expressed my surprise at how quickly she had done it. However, after several conversations with her in the coming weeks, we both knew that reconciliation was not a possibility. I had many people approaching me about reconciling with my wife and telling me to repent. My wife and I were at a place where neither of us wanted to reconcile.

Our conversations showed no sign of hope. I gave up on reconciliation, seeing it as a hopeless thing as well. My mood was filled with apathy, especially after being approached by so many who were telling me what was best for my life. I remember the words I wrote in a blog about this very personal issue:

> *"I think if we had lived in the land where everything works out, in the land where everyone reads James Dobson and watches Dr. Phil, where Mary Poppins cleans your house practically perfect in every way, where the black and white of Scripture never strays into the gray areas of life because nothing ever, ever works out wrong . . . our marriage would have worked out. But we didn't live there. I lived in a place where I fell, my wife didn't want me anymore, where I had cheated on her with a member of the church and her best friend, and she was done with me. She didn't want to reconcile. Did I? Not particularly."*

Over the next few months, I received many angry emails, text messages and other expressions of hurt from people. I would walk through department stores staring at the floor because I was afraid I might make eye contact with someone I knew. I was afraid of their scorn and anger. My shame was blaming me from within, the guilt was convicting my mind and the last thing I could handle were the looks from those I had harmed.

Sleep was a rare commodity in those days. I would lie awake at night with a heavy burden on my heart, thinking of my children, missing them. Allison and I would talk, she at her house and me in my rental home, separated by the miles. In those moments, I desperately wanted to stand before the church and beg for forgiveness. I didn't want to be a pastor again, I just wanted them to know how terrible I felt, how sorry I was. I grieved over the sin I had committed. I kept expecting each day that a church member might call and ask me how I was. If they called, I would have said, "I'm awful, I feel awful for what I did, please forgive me. I miss my mother. My heart is breaking. I need friends. I need prayer. I need support. Please help me." But the calls never came. I had hurt them badly.

Over time, I became angry because they did not call. I thought, "How dare they not care about me. I was by their sides when they had problems. I buried their dead. I married their children. I split up their fights! I preached for them. I taught them. I put together their services. I made bulletins. I served them the Lord's Supper and made sure their children had Vacation Bible School. And here I am wallowing in my misery and they can't even bear to make one phone call?" My anger boiled each day and night at them.

I had plenty of time to reflect on my sin and spent equal times blaming God and the church. It was a long time before I ever looked within for answers, realizing the blame belonged only to me. Even though I had these feelings, there was a relief of being out of the pastorate. There were no more expectations to meet, no more complaints, no more gossip, no more self-criticism.

There was also the moral and theological problem of being with Allison. My divorce wasn't final and I was carrying the scarlet letter of adultery. Allison and I didn't choose to be with each other because no one else would have us. We wanted to be together because we loved one another. Many people told us that our love was invalid and had no place in God's economy. I had many people telling me that in order to be repentant, I had to leave Allison for the rest of my life. I was told God would never be pleased with me again unless I left her. I tried to explain to these people that my wife and I were beyond reconciliation and that bridge had been crossed and burned. We moved forward, looking for a brighter time.

The Road Ahead

Within the year, my divorce was final and I immediately married Allison. I could feel God begin to work on my heart. Repentance came and began to quell the storm. Over a period of months, God began to break my heart and showed me the depth of my anger toward my former church members. I realized I was wrong and God began to convict me to approach several of them, including my former deacons, and ask for forgiveness.

One of the most touching conversations occurred with the church leader to whom I had to admit my adultery. I had wanted to talk to him for a long time, but it was almost two years later when we finally spoke. I met with him and sat with him in his pole barn. For ten minutes I poured out my soul and told him how sorry I was, and how I had acted stupid and prideful in the past two years. It was a very humbling experience, but it was necessary. He spoke to me with the grace he had always shown to me when I had pastored. He told me some things that had hurt him, but he was very kind as well. I knew our relationship would never be the same, but I also knew that it was a start.

Maybe I would never completely reconcile with my former church. However, I could make a start by taking my broken, humble heart and talking to the people I had hurt. In the interview process for my book, Dr. York had given me some good advice. He said that if a fallen pastor wants to be restored, "his repentance has to be more notorious than his sin."

I had started my blog hoping to clear my head and knew I would never return to ministry with such a broken soul. It was during that process that I realized that I had not embraced God's forgiveness for myself. I still hated myself for what I had done and was carrying around an immense amount of shame and self-hatred.

I began to search the Internet for fallen ministers and started emailing and calling them. Through my blog, broken ministers began to contact me about their own failures and asked for help. In those conversations, I learned that most congregations never forgive or reach out to reconcile with their former pastors. The forgiveness I longed for would apparently never materialize. It was a painful realization and I wrote about it in my blog one day:

> "I still felt like I deserved whatever anger church people threw at me. I wanted, however, the chance to stand before them and let them know how sorry I was. Yes, I could have done it at any time before I got found out. I realize that. Maybe my time had passed. But now, I wanted to face my sin and let them know. I had spent almost a decade there loving them, ministering. I had laid there at night knowing one thing was most assuredly true - any good that had come out of my time there, any people who had come to know Christ (which God gets credit for), any growth (again, which God

gets credit for), any late nights spent with church members who were sick, any hospital visits, any days spent in prayer - would all be lost. Because I would only be remembered as the pastor who committed adultery. And maybe that's how it should be."

Allison and I did find great solace through two churches that reached out to us and restored us. Both allowed us to attend and be ourselves. They accepted us and loved us for who we were. They loved on us and allowed us to rest, just being who God created us to be and not placing any demands upon us. In both of those churches, we were able to realize God's forgiveness and Christ's covering of our sin. I had almost lost complete faith in the church, but both congregations and their pastors gave us hope again.

The most healing thing that has occurred for me was the number of pastors who contacted me for advice before or after their fall. Through my blog, they reached out to me and asked me for help. Some told me that they felt no one else understood their plight except someone who had fallen. Some of them had not committed adultery yet and asked me what they should do. I told them they needed to reconcile with their wives and to avoid sin. One pastor said, "You didn't. What right do you have to tell me what to do?" I said, "My life isn't the moral standard to live by. Despite my sin, I do know that there are consequences for what we do. You know what the right thing to do is."

I've been able to talk to men who have just committed adultery and not yet told their wife or congregation. I advise them to be honest with their wife and tell her and to find help through counseling and seek restoration. I've talked to men who have fallen months ago and told them they need to find someone to walk with them through their pain. I think I knew God had humbled me greatly when the wife of a fallen pastor contacted me. She said he was unrepentant and she was struggling with forgiveness. I was heartbroken for her plight and was able to advise her about the pride and continued ways her husband would justify his sin. Through all those opportunities, I began to understand that God was not quite done using me and that His hand was still upon me to minister to others.

Pain and grief are two things that cannot be escaped. Over time, both of them have lessened in my life as I have sought to draw closer to understand the love of Christ. My subconscious wakes me weekly with dreams of me standing before them, preaching to them a sermon about my sorrow over failing them. Other times, I dream of a fellowship dinner with my former church and a happy, tearful reconciliation.

Within the days approaching the publication of this book, God has worked wonders in the reconciliation between me and several of my former church members. He is a gracious and sovereign God, who does indeed take our broken pieces and put them back together again for His glory. The good news is that our sin is never the end of the story thanks to Christ, the one who reaches out to the fallen in their most desperate hour.

There is hope that the culture in which we minister can be changed so other ministers can avoid such falls and traps. Only by understanding the problems surrounding us, the expectations that exist in ministry and the relationships within the church can we turn this situation around.

Section Two

Coming Alongside The Fallen Pastor

The problem in asking "why" is the fear of justifying the act. Reconciliation is virtually impossible in most situations because the prevailing church culture never wants to condone what originally happened. And instead of seeking our reconciliation and restoration, which are the hallmarks of the church, we ignore the problem hoping it will go away. It never does. The only way to answer the question is to face it and listen to it. But what if there was a clear story in Scripture that gave us a deeper sense of what it meant to restore?

Throughout my journey, I have found the most solace in the story of Christ's interaction with the adulterous woman in John 8. Before my fall, I did not care for it much. I looked upon the woman in the story and thought, "She deserves to have some sort of judgment passed on her, she sinned." But after my fall I was thirsty for grace and forgiveness. I found myself in the place of the adulterous woman, facing the angry crowd, wondering who my friend was.

When Jesus stood next to the adulterous woman in John 8, he was speaking directly to the prevailing Jewish culture. Adultery was punishable by death. But death wasn't the point. Restoration was. But he wasn't condoning adultery either. He would later tell her to turn from it. The angry mob had lined itself up demanding justice for her transgression, stones in hand. In standing with her, He was placing himself in harm's way. If the crowd throws the stone, they would hit him. And then Jesus uttered his famous words, "Let you without sin cast the first stone."

Christ stood between her and certain death, just as He would one day at Calvary. Jesus recognized that the only way towards reconciliation is to lay down our anger and judgment. The adulterous woman could not change what happened. But in laying down their stones they could embrace the grace and forgiveness that is the hallmark of the Kingdom of God.

Jesus had every right to judge her for her sin, but instead he showed compassion. He turned his criticism on those who would judge her and look down upon her. He was her only friend that day and He was the best friend she could have asked for. This is the reality of the fallen pastor.

What makes the fallen pastor's situation more serious is that he knew better. The voices in the crowd are stronger, the anger is intensified and the pain of the crowd is overbearing. Even then, Christ waits patiently for any sinner. His patient response is a model for any who would deal with a fallen sinner.

After my fall, I struggled to grasp the hand of Christ and stand to my feet. I felt I should stay ashamed of myself for the rest of my life. I thought it was my duty to hang my head in shame as long as I lived. I had failed my church, my children and my Savior. As time passed, I realized that Jesus would have none of that. His sacrifice was larger than my sin. His love was greater than anything I had done. His compassionate voice was louder than the crowd's: "Is anyone left to condemn you? Go and sin no more."

Forgiveness began with me. I began to reach out to fallen pastors across the country and talk to them about their experiences. I discovered that the circumstances that preceded their fall, the relationships they had and their lives after were strangely similar to mine. I had thought I was alone in my sin, but found that my situation was anything but atypical.

Each of these men had experienced a promising start to their ministries. Their marriages were good and some were starting new families. As they entered the church culture, their lives began to change. High expectations were placed upon them for success and tasks each week. They placed high expectations upon themselves and many of them worked excessively to meet those expectations. The pastor found his first mistress in the church, working hard for her, spending the majority of his time with her at the expense of the rest of his relationships. As those expectations rose, their relationship with their spouse got worse.

As their churches grew, they received affirmation from their churches, which gave them a temporary sense of satisfaction. Most felt they were being placed on a pedestal by their churches in a position where they could do no wrong. They were aware of their inherent weakness, but felt as if they were unable to show it. Some tended to exacerbate their ego so that no weakness could be seen in them.

As time went on, they stopped communicating with their spouses because they felt they were not able to share negative problems in church or they felt their spouses weren't as spiritual as they were. The ministry culture continued to wear down their marriage until intimacy was almost gone. The pastor found himself seeking affirmation from his church even more, driving himself harder at work to supplement the affirmation he was not getting at home.

For a few, a crisis or tragedy preceded the pastor's entering into an affair outside his marriage. But none of them were looking to get involved with another person. It appears that at the moment of contact with the other woman, each of them describes that their relationship with their church had soured somewhat. There had been a lack of appreciation or admiration for him and coupled with his marriage issues, he found himself to be needy.

Enter into the pastor's life another person with similar needs, not looking for an affair, but comfort of their own. Each relationship began with emotional attraction which accelerated quickly. Each pastor questioned himself during the process but came to an inevitable end, crossing the physical boundary. Each made the conscious decision to enter into temptation and suffer the consequences.

After each man was discovered, he was immediately removed from the church without any chance for counseling or much discussion. In each case, the church leadership was hurt and seemed to want to put the once idolized pastor out of the sight. The pastor left in his wake a hurt church with many questions, with little to no chance of reconciliation.

In the days that followed, few fellow ministers reached out to the fallen pastor. Long time friends were afraid to talk to him as they might be seen as being "guilty by association." Family members, parents, siblings often turned their back on him. The few people who did reach out to these men were often outsiders who said the same thing, "I love you. You messed up. It doesn't change who you are and I still love you."

A few of the pastors were able to reconcile with their wives and move beyond their sin. Others found themselves in the midst of divorce and child support hearings. Looking back at the sequence of events, most of them have asked, "How did I go from a pastor who loved Christ to adulterer?"

The process that leads to ministry failure builds over a period of time. But once the temptation to fall occurs, it happens so quickly that it is hard to understand. Many of these stories end with divorce and further sin, further compounding the problem. These stories are not patterns to be followed, but are presented to show the patterns that occur in the lives of fallen pastors to better understand the culture and the sin that follows and how to best respond and restore fallen pastors to Christian fellowship.

To discover "why" means listening to the stories that happen time and time again. And unless we address the issue head on, confronting the culture that plays a critical part in the process, we will never be able to seek out any kind of reconciliation. It is my hope that as we read the following stories, we can take the role that Christ did when he came alongside the woman in John 8. Christ wasn't looking to crown a "winner" in the argument between the adulterous woman and the angry mob. There was no winner to be found. He was looking to bestow compassion upon any who would follow him and listen to Him and His words and life of grace.

Chapter 3

Kris – "Who's The Man?"

Kris' experience was the perfect example of the culture that creates an idol. A dynamic personality experiences huge success that leads to an overwhelming sense of pride and crashes as a result.

Kris had been having an affair with Karla for four months. His suburban Toronto, Canada megachurch was thriving, but his marriage had been dead for years. However, his pride had convinced him that he could control the release of this scandal and he would be able to keep his job. He even knew how he was going to do it. The band would go silent, the room would be dark with only a little mood lighting and he would preach a stirring, yet intriguing sermon:

> *"I actually had a plan that I was going to get up on stage and preach a sermon called, 'Who's the Man.' That's how bad the sin in my life was. It was going to be about when David was confronted by Nathan and how I was the man who started this church. I'm the man who screwed up. I was going to confess. I was going to say, 'I'm going to be the man who continues to lead this church.' And in my mind, people were going to stand up and cheer and shout. How stupid is that? How stupid is sin? I justified it in my mind. I justified that God would allow me to have an affair because I was doing so much for Him and He knew my marriage was miserable."*

Kris had always been the kid who was told growing up that he would never amount to anything. He always had a chip on his shoulder. In his early youth, many would have thought their assumption was correct when he was deep into a life of sin and moral failure. Then he met his wife, Lynn who was a conservative Christian. "I went to church with her, God radically changed my life and I got saved. I knew immediately God was calling me into the ministry," he said. "That's what I wanted to do with my life. I got so focused."

Lynn had a troubled upbringing of her own and Kris was the first man she had ever been able to completely trust. She had a series of catastrophic events in her life and Kris helped her endure through them. However, from Kris' viewpoint, she was always emotionally distant from him: "She was not an emotional person. In ten years of marriage I never heard the words, 'I love you,' she never initiated a kiss. It just wasn't who she was." However, Kris' pre-conversion life had been the exact opposite and he recognized issues in his own life that led to worsening problems between them: "I was sexually active before I met her. I never tried to understand before why I sought affirmation in women." Instead of working on their marriage, Kris found satisfaction in his work:

> *"I worked all the time. She found her satisfaction in having children. When we planted our own church, it just grew and I became bigger and I worked all the time, travelled all the time. We were really just roommates at the end of the day. And during this time, my ego just got bigger and bigger."*

The church he planted in suburban Toronto grew from a handful of people to 1,500 in a year and a half. He had a dynamic personality coupled with a strong message and went after the unchurched population in the area. He was governed by a local group of pastors who had supported his church plant as a mission to the area. The church was considered non-traditional by most people's standards, but that was an inspiration to him and the members of his church. As they grew, he added a large band, preached from a large stage in his jeans and T-shirt, added several satellite campuses and his fame was beginning to grow in the northeast. He began to be viewed an expert on church planting in his region. The overwhelming success of Kris' church did not humble him. Instead, it empowered his ego:

> *"In that small town I lived in I was a rock star. I had armed security. We had a huge staff. Everywhere we went, people knew who we were. My ego got huge. I mean for the guy who was supposed to be a nobody growing up, I had become a big fish in a really small pond. The church fed my huge ego because I had multiple stages, standing ovations when I preached. It was just our church culture. So many of these people had given their lives to Christ in our church. They didn't know the proper way a man of God should act. It was us against the world at that church."*

As the church grew, he began to add staff. The staff he added was made up of a tight knit circle of friends. They helped build the church and bought into his vision, but they weren't people who held him accountable in his spiritual life:

> *"No one was going to keep me accountable, they're all getting paid. No one's going to challenge me on anything. What it boiled down to was my ego was so huge."*

The pressure of pastoring, speaking and being on a large stage also left Kris with feelings of burnout. At the time, he didn't realize it, but he was going non-stop seven days a week building his church, his ministry and making a name for himself. He had placed high expectations on himself, felt high expectations from the church as well as local pastors:

> *"I look back now and see how fried and burned out I was. Our church had gotten to the point where I wasn't really doing ministry. There were expectations of other pastors. The weekly draw. How many got saved, how many are you running, who's the biggest and the best, who's the latest and the greatest. The pressure from that was crazy. I look back at that time at my previous church and I never enjoyed anything. I never stopped and enjoyed folks getting saved. It was never enough. I was living on energy drinks and fast*

food. I was burned out. I was sleeping three hours a night. I
was like a crack addict without the crack. I was destined to
crash and when I crashed, it was huge."

As the church grew, his relationship with his wife diminished severely. He was finding acceptance at church from his staff and the standing ovations from his parishioners, but no intimacy from his spouse. This caused a deeper rift within his marriage. He would stand on stage with the lights and band surrounding him and find no marriage relationship at home:

"But when I came home, I was a nobody. That was a big
adjustment for me. All day long I was somebody in the
community. I could come home and I wouldn't get a 'hello.'
So instead of me working on my marriage and trying to get
my wife to love me, I just retreated to my email and to my
phone to try and help other pastors and church planters
where I was somebody."

In hindsight, Kris knows when he began to slide for the worse. Despite his ego spinning out of control, he still had set mental and physical boundaries for himself. He said, "I had the rules set in place. I never traveled alone. I was never alone with a woman. The heart wasn't right but the boundaries kept me from falling." Most likely, his principles were the only thing that kept him from falling sooner than he did. Mentally, however, he admits that he began to sin.

"It really started for me with fantasy. It was always,
'Everything else is great, but my marriage is terrible. But
things would be different if I was just married to that lady.'
You start playing that 'what if' game in your mind."

Kris' need for affirmation grew each day. He began to work out to lose weight, began to buy expensive clothes to wear and increased his online presence:

"It was about me and my ego."

All of his energy was put forth toward his ministry and his presence within the church.

"The whole time I'm not working on my marriage. Never turning my heart towards her, never putting her first, always complaining that she should be all about me. She should serve me."

Kris said that looking back, his wife seemed content in their marriage taking care of the kids and living her dream to be a mother.

In his sixth year, Kris had assumed a CEO type role in his church. It was very difficult for church members to contact him and his staff made all the decisions for him. During that time, the staff hired a new children's minister, Karla. Despite the fact that Kris had never been tempted and he had kept his rules of boundary in place, he was immediately taken with Karla:

"She was beautiful and had a heart for ministry. She was everything in my mind my wife wasn't."

They saw each other daily and their feelings for one another seemed mutual. They began flirting with one another when they saw each other. Even though they were never alone with one another, both knew something was happening. Things quickly accelerated when Karla came to see Kris for advice:

"One day she came to me to tell me her marriage was falling apart. She wanted to let me know as a pastor and as a staff member. And for the first time ever – you have that defining moment where you look back – I opened myself up and made a joke. I said, 'Under different circumstances, we would have made a great couple.' That just fuels it when it makes you feel like a little teenager all of a sudden. Then you become consumed with that person."

From that moment, they were consumed with one another. It was purely emotional for a while as they discussed the "what ifs" of life and lived in a fantasy of what could be:

"She thought I was the perfect guy. She didn't know that I leave my underwear lying around the house, that I'm a selfish pig. She just saw the guy on the stage. She thought, 'That's what I want for my life.'"

Their mutual attraction continued and they crossed the physical line when they shared their first kiss. After that, then began to plan how they were going to consummate their relationship. When they finally did, they kept their love secret successfully for four months. Kris recalls his spiritual decline after their relationship began in earnest.

> *"I was spiritually unhealthy. I remember the first Sunday preaching after I started my affair. I walked up on stage, soaking in sweat, and I said to God, 'God, just kill me while I'm on stage.' But then after that, it just became normal."*

The pressure got worse and worse for Kris and Karla. He knew his staff and Lynn had suspicions about his relationship with Karla, so he approached his leadership and told them he and Lynn were having marriage problems. The staff responded with an exclusive weekend marriage retreat for Christian couples to Niagara Falls by train the next weekend. He and Lynn left for the retreat but he had no intention of healing his marriage. More importantly, while they were gone, Kris' staff went through his desk and found printed out email correspondence between he and Karla. On the final day of the retreat, the staff phoned Lynn and told her of Kris' infidelity:

> *"You know that feeling when you can look at someone who's on the phone and know what they're being told? I don't know why they couldn't have waited until we got back. That was it. We were never together again. I don't know that we could have ever gotten back together, but any hope of us getting back together was ruined at that point. Let me make it clear I take total responsibility. It was all me."*

When they arrived, Kris was asked for his resignation by the leadership and he moved out upon the request of Lynn. The church staff was obviously hurt and angry over his sin and rallied around Lynn. It's been said that in situations like Kris', people need someone to love and someone to hate. Such sensitive matters tend to be very polarizing, even in the Christian community. He said:

*"The staff made people choose sides. Either people had to
be for my ex-wife or for me. And if you had anything to do
with me, it was viewed as a slap in the face to my ex-wife."*

The staff surrounded Lynn like Kris' personal security used to surround him
each day, not letting him anywhere close to her or his children:

*"I couldn't call her. I couldn't do anything. They changed
the locks on the doors. All of a sudden I was the devil. They
handled a lot wrong, but they didn't know what they were
doing, in their defense."*

Lynn filed for divorce and so did Karla. The church was going through an
intense time of hurt and Kris began spiraling downward into his own world
of pain and depression. He and Karla were living together, waiting for the
public anger to quell. It was during this time that God began to work on
Kris and his heart. Nine months later, he received an email from a local
pastor that said, "God loves you and I'd love to have you come look at our
church one day." Kris assumed that the pastor wanted his advice on how to
improve his church attendance or growth. However, Kris said that when he
and Karla showed up one Sunday:

*"They just loved on us. I was kind of offended that they didn't
ask me for advice. I still had a little pride in me."*

Kris said the church needed a lot of work. The music was poor, the programs
needed help and there was a lot of room for overall improvement. But they
never asked for his help.

*"Every Sunday, we just showed up at that church and they
loved on us. It was during this time that my divorce was
final. For the first time I began to work on my own issues."*

Kris had found refuge in a place where nothing was expected of him, but
he was given time to rest and be restored by God. He and Karla met with
a counselor for an extended period of time to help him through issues he
knew existed well before he ever became a pastor.

After a period of time, Kris started a local Bible study that a few people attended. After a year or so, 200 people were attending. He says they didn't advertize:

> *"Advertizing for me just triggers like an addict. If I start to advertize it starts triggering for me to want to be the biggest and the best."*

His church meets in a public area in a worn out part of town and Kris knows he's a different minister now.

> *"For the first time ever I have a daily quiet time with God. I know that sounds crazy, but before I was always looking for a sermon. I'm not trying to impress people. I'm not worried about who shows up. We're just trying to reach hurting people."*

He and Karla married and have found a rich relationship through all the adversity. He says he still fights against his own issues in regard to respecting women, but has definitely come a long way. He says he knows he'll always live with the consequences with what he did for the rest of his life, but is thankful for the blessings he has now.

Chapter 4

Paul – An Emotional Affair

Paul's story is different than the other fallen pastors. He committed emotional adultery and faced the problems the other pastors did, but before falling into physical adultery with Marleigh, a staff member, he approached his church for help. He felt he was doing the right thing by seeking counsel from the church leadership, but discovered that his problems were just beginning:

> "Here's how I would describe it – I committed emotional,
> spiritual and intellectual adultery. I never touched her in any
> inappropriate way but I was spent."

Instead of taking the final plunge into physical adultery, he and Marleigh decided to trust the church leadership group and ask for help. Paul confessed the depths of his feelings for Marleigh to his wife Dana. Then both he and Marleigh went to the leadership team. In private, they told the team the details of the problem and asked them for help in coping with their problems and asked them what they should do as leaders and Christians. The leadership team convened and made their decision. The leadership team decided to keep the details of the emotional affair concealed, place Paul on administrative leave, send he and Dana to a counselor, and keep Marleigh on staff full-time. It was business as usual at the church. Paul was disappointed in the staff's decision:

> "The way they chose to help, they chose to keep everything
> hidden under the rug basically and said, 'You go away and

you go see a counselor. We'll pay for the counselor. You get better then you come back.'"

Paul was shocked and disappointed at the decision of the leadership team, mostly made of people whom he considered friends and trusted. He said:

"It was if the church was embarrassed to actually find a sinner on their staff. They were upset because it happened right under their noses."

Paul had already been through a terrible set of circumstances. His father had died a year before, which caused him overwhelming grief. Now, he was preparing to speak to his leadership team about an emotional affair he was involved in. The death of his father had been the most trying time of Paul's life. He had felt that none of the leadership team had pursued opportunities to walk beside him in his grieving process. This had bothered him deeply, especially since he had been the one who had counseled and mentored many in the church during their times of trouble. In that year, he had been through many stressful times at the church, but the loss of his father had been one of the heaviest burdens on his soul.

Paul was a well-respected associate pastor in his late 30s serving at a large, seeker-friendly church in the suburbs of Minneapolis. On an average Sunday, the attendance was well over 400. Paul had found his calling serving as minister over small groups at the church. He spent hours poring over meticulous details and making sure things were being done the right way. He often felt the pressures from the church to meet expectations, but even worse were his own expectations which exceeded any the leadership team placed upon him. Whatever project was placed before him, he was zealous in its perfection and completion.

His greatest accomplishment was the mentoring program he had started. He was responsible for mentoring a group of men and training them to replicate the same ministry to others. To the church, he was the spiritual mentor and counselor that many came to for advice and help in times of turmoil. Unfortunately, when the men he had trained were released to do their own mentoring and counseling, they were unable to reach out to Paul and attend to his grief or see that he was dealing with issues of his own:

> *"They still looked at me as a mentor or a spiritual father figure, a pastor. They weren't able to carry me or confront me because they weren't there yet at that point."*

Paul was suddenly isolated from the group that had been so close to him for many years. His wife, Dana, who was employed as the executive pastor's secretary, had some of the same frustrations he was feeling as well. They had trouble communicating about their issues and had lost some of the intimacy they had once shared together.

> *"My wife working in the church almost created a barrier because we weren't supposed to talk about church because her boss was on a peer level with me on the leadership team. And work was our life."*

One of the other issues facing their marriage was the depth of their spiritual relationship. Paul felt that Dana and he had always had trouble connecting on the things of God throughout their marriage:

> *"One of the struggles that my wife and I have had, all of our married life; we did a great job raising kids, we dealt with money tremendously, sex was fine, all that kind of stuff was cool. But the connection spiritually, emotionally, intellectually; my wife's always been intimidated by my spirituality. I think it's more my speed in processing things and thinking through things. It takes her a little longer to process."*

With all of these events, Paul had unknowingly grown into a place of isolation, despite the many friendships he had carefully cultivated by networking within the church. His marriage wasn't unserviceable, but it was stagnant and seemed to be unfruitful. He later realized how tired he had become and had lost much of his zest for ministry. He said:

> *"I got to a point where I was just pretty empty."*

During this time, the church hired Marleigh, a new staff member to facilitate the increased work load that Paul was experiencing in his department. Marleigh found instant happiness working in the small groups department and loved the vision that Paul casted. She immediately offered to help Paul with his ideas for the church and her hours were increased to help Paul with his work. As they collaborated together on the small group project, Paul and Marleigh grew into a closer relationship and his work benefited from it:

> "We were working all the time and we had organized out the plan for all the ministry responsibilities that I had. She was helping me become very productive. We were connecting so well, working so well together, carrying each other. More productive than I've ever been in my life. I just got to a point where the things that I struggled with my wife, the spiritual connection, the emotional connection and the intellectual stuff and even the vocational side of things, we just clicked. She could also understand people like my wife and was almost a translator for both sides."

At first, it was a working relationship as they spent many hours together on the small group project. The hours sped by as they shared life stories, personal issues, hopes and dreams. Paul began to share lunch breaks with Marleigh and her husband Richie, who also worked at the church. During those breaks, Marleigh would openly talk about the troubling issues in her marriage and Paul would try to help Richie see what he was missing:

> "It really got to a point where she and I were having these great conversations with her husband and her husband wasn't aware, even though he was right there. I even got to the point where I was trying to help him see what he was not doing or seeing and he would just resist me."

Paul began to realize he was taken with Marleigh and he could sense it was mutual. He couldn't wait to get to work each day to see her:

> "I couldn't get her out of my head. I tried to fight it. She tried to fight it."

To complicate matters, Marleigh was also becoming good friends with Dana at church. Paul spoke frequently of Marleigh but it apparently raised no suspicions:

> *"I didn't try to hide my obsession with her from my wife, but I*
> *did hide (Marleigh's) obsession with me from her."*

Their relationship continued to grow and both of them were aware of the consequences if things went beyond an emotional level. They were aware that they had crossed an inappropriate emotional line but continued to talk in private, feeding the other's need for an emotional and spiritual connection. The tensions continued to rise with no end in sight so they agreed to meet at a park after work one afternoon and seriously discuss the future of their relationship. Both of them spoke openly with the other and came to the conclusion that they needed to fight the temptation before they crossed the line into physical adultery. Their obsession had created an almost impossible working environment:

> *"One day I would fight it and she wouldn't be. The next, she*
> *would be fighting it and I wouldn't be."*

They spent the next month in complete frustration, fighting their temptations and urges - and at the end of it, both were emotionally and spiritually spent. Paul also admits that at that time he was ready to take Marleigh away, abandon the ministry and spend the rest of his life with her. He was a broken man who had found comfort in someone else to confide in.

That was the moment he and Marleigh decided to approach the church leadership for guidance. After they decided to send him away for counseling to solve this huge issue, Paul knew there was a basic problem with the way the church was handling things. Paul recognized that the church staff was completely unequipped for such a situation, especially since he normally would have been the staff member helping someone in his situation.

After three months of counseling, Paul returned to his work on a Monday to find that his desk was within ten feet of Marleigh's. The leadership team was still silent about the issue and had placed restrictions on their interaction together. Marleigh and Paul were not to speak about anything except work related items and even then, they were to keep it at a minimum. Paul knew members of the leadership team were keeping a close eye on him. He discovered the reason the church leadership had swept the issue under the rug was because they thought if the congregants had learned of his emotional infidelity, "marriages across the church would have fallen apart." A member of the leadership team told him that he was sent away to protect the members of the church.

"I felt like a leper."

Things did not improve for Paul and Marleigh. Despite the strict rules in place, the desires were still there. For three days in a row after work, they had conversations at a local coffee shop about their feelings and the reality of their situation. Knowing once again that their passions were strong, they told the leadership team that they both needed help and needed to be separated in the workplace. The leadership team refused and offered Paul the option of going through the same three months of counseling. He could then return to the workplace just as things were.

Paul confronted the leadership team and said:

> *"You don't seem to understand. Marleigh and I cannot be in the same place. We have an intellectual and spiritual addiction to one another and must be separated. We are coming to you for help."*

The leadership team appeared either blind to the problem or resigned to hide the issue from the rest of the church. Realizing the problem wouldn't change, Paul resigned immediately but Marleigh stayed on staff to continue her work small group ministry.

Paul left angry, confused and bitter, wondering why his pleas for help had gone unanswered and why the church seemed to be favoring Marleigh. He tried repeatedly to call the church and those involved, but no one would speak with him. Finally, three months after leaving, he walked into the church office to ask for an explanation. He was met at the doors by the head of the leadership council who Paul suggested "blocked his way and got in his face." Paul was looking for answers, but the church leadership was looking to put the story behind them. The church leader finally said to Paul:

> *"Just because you destroyed your own life, why do you think you have to destroy everyone else's?"*

Paul has had a chance to examine the incidents of the past and has found healing through time and counseling. When asked how the church leadership might have handled the incident differently and how other churches might learn from his experience, he said:

> *"I wish they would have gone to the congregation and told them the truth. I wish the leadership would have said, 'We love these people and we're going to try to bring them back and restore them like they've carried us and helped us when we needed it.'"*

Unfortunately, the situation was completely opposite:

> *"Instead they kept it hidden among the leadership. They didn't look for outside help. They had no idea what to do with me."*

Paul still works through the incidents that occurred in his life years ago. While he broke the bond of trust with his wife and his church, he felt like he did the right thing in approaching the church leadership in asking for help. There is still a bitterness that resonates with Paul who desperately needed someone to walk with him in his most troubling time as he walked with people before.

Chapter 5

Dathan – Twice Fallen

Dathan thought he had put the pieces back together. He had cheated on his wife and been removed from his ministry. After their divorce, he had moved back home, joined a church and had repented. He was doing everything right – or so he thought. But every time he looked around, people were judging him, talking about him, never giving him a chance. He finally threw in the towel and descended further into sin.

His life became an overwhelming anthem written daily against the God he once loved. Dathan's anger continued to grow over time and he began to hate everyone and everything that came between his feud with God. He reserved his worst hatred for God and became entrapped within it. He began and ended his day with vile, spewing, profane hate for the God he once revered, worshiped and adored:

> *"I spent a year where every night that I went to bed I begged God and asked him to let me die in my sleep and take me home. And every morning I woke up and was madder than a wet hen. I would cuss God for letting me live. This went on for a year. At the end of one year, I was in my apartment, I decided and I sat down and talked to God and said, 'You are no longer my Father, I am no longer your son, we are divorced. I hate you and that's it. I'm done with you. I will never speak of you again.' Except with a lot of profanity. From that point on, I quit the morning/night thing and just went off and was angrier than before."*

How could this God whom he once adored lead him to this place? He had tried desperately to pick up the pieces and yet church people had descended upon him like buzzards to pick apart the pieces. How had he gone from dynamic associate pastor to a man at odds with his Creator? The story began almost a decade before.

Dathan could still smell Carol's perfume on him as he pulled his SUV into the church parking lot. There wasn't supposed to be another car here, and it definitely wasn't supposed to be the pastor's. It was close to midnight and Dathan, associate pastor of youth and education, had just consummated a long time relationship with Carol, one of his church members. They had driven thirty minutes away into the dark Mississippi night and connected in what seemed to be a magical way for both of them. For six months, they had been exchanging glances, passing notes, and eventually kissed several times. Dathan loved Carol for everything she was able to give him. Yet, Dathan was broken and he didn't realize it.

How had he ended up in this position? He and his wife Anita hadn't been sexually intimate in a long time and Dathan had caught himself fantasizing about other women thinking:

> "'I wonder what it would be like to be with her?' He loved Anita, but confessed that even since he had married her, "I wasn't in love with her. And I know that's terrible. I was resolved to the fact that this was where I was for the rest of my life. I was stuck."

He didn't want to be married anymore, but that didn't mean he was out looking for a reason to cheat. He figured he would be married to his wife Anita forever, since divorce meant being cast out of the ministry. He knew the truth:

> "You don't divorce in ministry. You don't commit adultery."

Yet, he found himself being drawn to Carol, a young woman who understood him and responded to him and his needs.

Dathan's church had been wonderful to him. The expectations upon him had been high, but he had taken it in stride. He had always loved the ministry and probably would have done his job for free. He loved serving the church and his zeal and passion drove his heart to work harder each week. He had excelled at his job, doing the best he could to please the church he loved so much. Of course, there were always certain groups of people who placed unrealistic expectations upon him, wanting more, but he had been able to put them out of his mind for the most part. Dathan also knew that he had struggled his whole life with a bent towards some sort of sexual sin. It was hard to describe, but he knew that it was lurking in his soul:

> *"Early on, there was something there – a bent in my life that I had a propensity towards something like that happening, a seed of sin. I knew it, but I didn't know it. It's hard not to recognize that being there but you don't really think about how harmful it can be down the road."*

He also realized another factor that led to his fall. He had led a life of legalism and judgmentalism:

> *"My relationship with the Lord was based on rules of do's and don'ts, not love. Did I love the Lord? Yes. But my motivation was because it was the right thing to do."*

Dathan stated if the command from the Bible was to love his brothers and sisters in the Lord, he did it not out of joy or love, but because that was the command. If the Bible commanded he tithe, he put his money in the plate not out of joy, but out of duty. Everything he did was based on a harsh system of black and white rules with absolutely no gray areas. He said there was very little authentic love in his relationship with God and as soon as he got married, that bled into the relationship with his wife. He loved his wife because it was his Scriptural mandate to do so. When Carol came into his life, it opened a new world he had never considered:

> *"When this woman came along, and I fell head over heels in love, the rules of do's and don'ts soon became overpowered by the fact that I was in love with a woman. And it wasn't enough to follow the rules anymore."*

And now, he had been caught. The pastor was waiting for Dathan in the parking lot. A thousand things rolled through Dathan's mind, but he knew why Brother Roger was there. He hoped it was something else, but he began to prepare a story and a defense before he even got out of his SUV. He was still trying to justify what had just taken place while he walked over to the pastor.

Brother Roger didn't hesitate, "You've been with Carol."

"What are you talking about?" Dathan thought he could keep it together, but he immediately realized he was wrong.

"Just come with me into my office. Anita is there too," Brother Roger said turning on his heels to go into the church.

When he walked into the office, he saw his wife Anita, eyes stained with tears. She looked betrayed, angry, yet broken. Dathan had stopped complete intimacy with her from the moment he had kissed Carol four months before. Anita had been aware there were problems, but Dathan had blamed them on ministry problems and Anita had shown patience. However, Anita had suspected something was going on and began to talk to Brother Roger.

As soon as everyone sat down, Brother Roger began to accuse and question Dathan. Every accusation and penetrating question was precise. Dathan decided his best plan of action would be to say nothing. Usually a talkative, energetic person, Dathan completely shut down. He listened for two hours as the pastor talked and demanded a confession. Dathan refused. The pastor immediately dismissed him from his job and put a plan together to get him out of the community and move the entire family back to Michigan. The plan was formulated by the church leadership to fly Carol and the kids back to her parent's home in Detroit while Dathan stayed to pack and wait for a family member from Lansing to drive to Mississippi with a moving truck. The church paid for Dathan to stay in a local hotel while he waited for three days for his family member to arrive.

During the three-day wait, he and Carol took advantage of their waning time together in the hotel. He figured that since he had already fallen so far, there was little he could do to slip any further. There was a bond between them that he didn't want to lose and each moment they spent together made time stand still. However, the bond had to be broken and several days later, he left for Lansing to stay with a family member. After getting settled, he stayed in close phone contact with Carol. His family member discovered his sin and was disappointed with him. They were even less happy when it was discovered that he was still communicating with Carol. When his sin was laid bare, the family member demanded he stop or he find somewhere else to live. Dathan chose to move out.

He found a 400 square foot apartment, 100 square feet of which had apparently already been rented out by cockroaches. The disappointment was strong across his family:

> *"Someone told me later that my younger brother told them that I was his hero and that he said, 'my hero fell.'"*

His parents wouldn't speak to him, he had begun uncontested divorce proceedings on his wife, and eventually, he and Carol stopped speaking. He struggled to find work and was at the lowest point in his life, feeling completely abandoned, but knowing he had deserved what had happened. Some of his old friends in Michigan would stop by to talk to him.

> *"They came 'at me.' I think they thought they were trying to help me the best they knew how. But most of them were still angry about what I had done and were demanding repentance from me, but their words meant nothing to me. I didn't hear concern. I only heard judgment. Most of my friends from seminary and the ministry never called. Only two ever reached out they pretty much said, 'you're done, buddy.'"*

For the rest of his onetime pastor friends, not calling makes some sense to him now:

> *"To have anything to do with me would be to condone my actions."*

While back in Michigan among people who knew him, Dathan turned his heart toward God and repented. He sought out help from a local church:

> *"I was trying to do everything right."*

Unfortunately, his every move was being watched:

"There was a severe scrutiny to see if I had actually repented."

Dathan said everyone was watching to see if he had actually changed. Few would speak to him or approach him. He ended up in a treacherous cycle in the local churches who found little room for him or the sin he had committed:

> *"Even when I got back into church, everything was fine until they found out in the church I was in what I had done and then they didn't want to have anything to do with me. I'd switch churches and the same thing would happen."*

As this rejection continued, he said that he began to feel drug down again. His second downfall was eminent:

> *"Then, Satan snuck in and said, 'they're never going to forgive you.'"*

He finally grew tired of the Christian community's rejection and gave up altogether. His second slide into sin was worse than the first and lasted several years. Dathan explained he tried to walk the right path after his first fall, but felt rejected by the church:

> *"I don't blame them even though they were wrong. I don't hold them accountable for that. I hold myself accountable for what I did. Seven years I'm responsible for no matter what they were doing. I'm responsible for my sins and actions. But that's what Satan used – their lack of forgiveness."*

Over the next six years, Dathan continued in a downward spiral away from God. One of the people most disappointed in Dathan was his father, Jessie. Jessie was a hard working man who rarely showed physical or emotional affection toward Dathan, but loved him deeply. On the night of his ordination, his father said to someone in the church, "This is my most proud moment of my son." Dathan heard of his dad's comment years later and asked him, "Dad, why didn't you tell me that? I would have loved that." His dad replied, "I just thought you knew."

After his failure in the ministry, his father stopped speaking to him completely. His dad worked as the principal at the middle school where

Dathan's children attended. When Dathan would come pick them up at school, Jessie would see Dathan coming and make a slow jog away from him just to avoid him.

> *"It was so he wouldn't have to look upon me. Like he was saying, 'I'm done with you.'"*

It would take a full six years before his parents could find room to forgive him for his sin. His parents had been so proud of him, their expectations of him and his future, and the let down had been severe.

He plunged further into sin and hardened his position against God, his family and anyone who tried to reach out to him. He describes himself as a "24/7-rageaholic madman":

> *"Everything made me mad. It made me mad to have to get up and brush my teeth. It made me mad to get my keys out of my pocket and start the car."*

Dathan was determined to run from God in his anger but now realizes that God has a patient approach with His children:

> *"He's impeccable and he's going to respond to you in the perfect way. But he's going to respond to us differently because we're all different. But he won't change. He will respond to fallen pastors differently because they're all different."*

It was during this time that Dathan ended his days with angry tirades against God, desiring death and eventually asking for separation from Him. In asking for that separation, though, Dathan found something he had not counted on. He found a God who was patiently waiting. Dathan points to Psalm 51, David's Psalm of repentance after committing sin with Bathsheba when referring to this time in his life. He especially quotes verse 8: "Let the bones you have broken rejoice." Dathan describes this time as God breaking him down and pulling him back to a place of repentance:

> *"Everything in my life just got worse then. My life was like an old fashioned pressure cooker. It was like God put me in one of those. Looking back, that's what had to happen.*

*For me to be of any value, I had to have everything stripped
of me, every negative thing stripped from me and crushed
and destroyed. The entire time it made me angry. It took
my sleep, my health, and my personality. God crushed my
body physically. I couldn't think or talk, or do basic functions.
It was God taking his child – if you are a Christian and you
truly are his child and you stray, he is coming to get his child,
because he loves you. He allowed me to stay here on earth
and wallow with the pigs in the far country."*

Dathan had turned into the prodigal son, the one who had run as far as his
own strength could carry him and it had exhausted him. One day, he found
himself in a pitiful state in a woman's house. The woman thought he was
in such bad shape that she called Dathan's parents, with whom she had
no prior relationship. She told them, "I don't know what's wrong with him,
but you better come get him." Dathan describes his state of mind that day
similar to the prodigal son:

*"When you read the prodigal son, it says he came to his
senses. That means he lost his senses."*

His parents retrieved him and he spent 30 days there. His parents had not
had much contact with him over the years and had no idea what to do with
him but be patient. During those days, he finally did come to his senses
and repented of his sin. He was in the house he had grown up in, entered
his sister's old room, laid his forehead on the floor, stretched his arms out
wide and waited for the mercy of God and had a 45 minute restoration
experience with God. He discussed part of a very personal experience in
which he felt the forgiveness of God:

*"It was an experience I will never forget. It wasn't anything
I did, all I did was talk. When I hit the ground, all I said was,
'I'm sorry.' I had nothing left of me but to fall on the floor,
willfully and just say, 'I'm sorry, please forgive me, will you
take me back?' God had done all these things, but he left my
will there because he's not going to force me to love him. He
allowed me, even though he did everything to bring me back
to love him, to say, 'I want to be back. I love you.' I didn't have*

anything within me but to say, 'I'm sorry.' Once that was said to Him with honesty and sincerity and sincere repentance, he did everything else. And I sat back and watched with my eyes closed but it was something I've never seen in my entire life. It scared my parents to death. We talked about it years later and my mom said, 'please don't ever do that to me again.'"

Dathan began to attend a local church and continued his restoration process. There, he met Jocelyn, who he began to date. He wondered how he would tell her about his past but finally felt it was the right time after they had been seeing each other for a while.

"When I finally told her, she said, 'Isn't it good that God is the master of timing?' She had already fallen in love with me, and I suppose some women still could have taken off. But God put us together."

Today they are happily married and Dathan has God's call upon his life to reenter the ministry. On occasion, he has the opportunity to share his testimony with groups of pastors and men on the dangers of being prideful and how to avoid the pitfalls of ministry failure. He is fulfilled with his current life but knows that there will always be repercussions for his sin and warns ministers of the sins of the seventh commandment: "I have been forgiven for my adultery, but there are consequences that continue over two decades later."

Chapter 6

Shannon – Great Was The Fall

Shannon's story shows an example of how a man who ministers can go from great respect to town outcast in a matter of hours. Shannon and his first wife had problems for years, but it was never seen by the community. He immersed himself into his study and eventually broke, opening his heart for temptation. Over a decade later, many of those who followed him and trusted him still refuse to speak to him.

Shannon stood at his mother's grave for hours that day, weeping. He had nowhere else to go. Earlier that day, he had been viewed as a well-respected Sunday school teacher, known throughout the community. Within a few hours, his sin with Pam had been discovered and he was now an outcast.

> *"It was a terrible day. 8 million people were looking for me.*
> *I just went out to my mother's grave and sat out there and*
> *cried. When it got dark, I finally went to Pam's house."*

Shannon had experienced a fall from a great height and knew it. Many people had depended on his teaching of the Bible for comfort and education. Decades later, he is still a pariah in his community to many for what he did and he still struggles with the pain he caused his family and his former church.

Twenty hours a week is a lot of time to spend preparing for a thirty-minute sermon every Sunday. It's an even more significant number of hours when you consider it's how much time Shannon Smith spent preparing to teach his Sunday school lesson each week. Shannon was a perfectionist when it came to detail and teaching. He said it took him eight months to take his class through the book of Ephesians and a year through the book of Revelation.

> *"I was big on the details. As soon as I was done teaching one week, I was already thinking about next week's lesson."*

When Shannon took over the class at First Baptist Rapid City, it had only seven members. From there, it grew to seventy members and was being broadcast locally over the radio. The class members loved the practical way he drew out the truth of Scripture.

> *"If there was something there most people read over, it stuck out to me and I just had to chase the rabbit."*

There were high expectations for Shannon at First Baptist to excel as a teacher and carry his load. He internalized this pressure and stress and expected more of himself than the leadership ever could.

Many times, he was approached about being a deacon, but he never felt worthy, despite the fact that most people in the church saw him as a role model and a mentor.

> *"I always felt that those guys were 'up there.' I just didn't compare."*

He also had high expectations placed upon him by his in-laws.

> *"No one was ever good enough for their daughter. My wife would always exclaim, 'What do you want? He's at church every time the doors are open and he teaches Sunday school!'"*

He and his wife Dorothy had always struggled with sexual and spiritual intimacy. Shannon stated that she never had an equal interest in religion that he had so there was always something lacking between them.

> *"One thing that disappointed me about her, she never read her Bible. It was almost like her religion rode on my coattails."*

They never had any major conflicts, but seemed to merely share living space for 20 years of marriage. Shannon admits that because of this, he had a lot of unfulfilled sexual needs and desires for the majority of their marriage.

Pam was a member of Shannon's class and had been divorced for ten years after a troubled marriage. He had known her for several years, but had never had any serious attraction to her. Pam had been divorced for almost a decade and had not dated anyone during that time. She had been faithful to church and was very careful about choosing her friends. Shannon explained Pam's life before she met him:

> "She had been hurt real bad so she didn't give herself to anybody on a relationship basis. She would go home from church, read her Bible and go to bed. She told me, 'The only one I really trust is the Lord.' She had a love affair with the Lord."

However, as his marriage began to rapidly deteriorate, Shannon began talking to Pam after class and was attracted to her dedication to the Bible and to the Lord:

> "We could talk, but there was never really anything serious beyond that. My intentions were good at that point."

One week, Dorothy left to visit family in Illinois. Shannon was talking to Pam after class about his love for walking around town each day, and asked if she wanted to join him. That day, they began a regular routine of walking together.

> "That's when things started to click."

He also realized that he was putting himself in a situation where he could get into trouble, especially since he had problems at home.

> "I knew better. I realized I was putting myself in that situation."

As their time together increased, so did their emotional intimacy. During a walk, Shannon told Pam, "People have to be careful because you reach a place where you cross a point of no return." About a month later, they were in church on a Wednesday night, sitting close to one another and

Pam passed a note to Shannon. On the note she had written, "I think I've passed that point of no return."

Following that evening service, they went out to a local restaurant for coffee and he confessed to her that he had crossed that line in his mind as well. They decided to consummate their relationship physically. They were able to carry on their affair for almost a year secretly. Shannon continued to teach and Pam continued to come to Sunday school.

> *"We were living a lie. I was still teaching, I was teaching truth, but I was living a lie."*

Dorothy was becoming suspicious and those suspicions were confirmed when she saw Shannon and Pam together at a restaurant. She confronted Pam and Shannon separately and neither of them confirmed nor denied it. Shannon became tired of hiding for so long.

> *"I said to myself, 'That's it. I've lived the lie as long as I can live it.'"*

He left Dorothy a note on the kitchen table, packed up his Bible, what he could fit in a suitcase and left. He met Pam at a restaurant and said, "You remember you promised to put me up if the world came crashing down?" Pam nodded her head. "Well, it has." He moved in with Pam immediately. In a matter of hours, in the eyes of the community, he would go from respected radio Sunday school teacher to adulterer.

The fallout was tremendous. Many people stopped by Pam's house to try to talk him out of it including several friends and family. They all had different motives.

> *"I had one guy stop by and we had lunch, but I think he was nosier than anything. He wasn't a true friend, as such."*

Shannon and Pam had one couple that reached out in authentic friendship toward them.

> *"I went to see a close church friend of mine the day I left. I told him the story. He said, 'Shannon, I don't understand it. But I love you, you're my friend.' And he was. His wife called me a scoundrel, but she said, 'I love you.' And I could go to*

> *their house. They would invite us out for holidays. We didn't*
> *have anybody but them."*

The pastor stopped by to tell him to repent. He told him the only way for him to be justified in God's eyes was to leave Pam, but Shannon's mind was made up. He had made his decision to be with Pam. She did for him what no one had ever done before. She met his every need in every way and he was exhausted from trying to hide. The next day, he went to the church, handed in his keys to the secretary.

> *"I said to her, 'I'm not going through this church discipline*
> *aspect. I want our names taken off the church roll right now.*
> *We're guilty and we don't want to bring any more disgrace*
> *upon the church than we already have.'"*

It took a year for the divorce finalize between Dorothy and him. His family was angry with him for a long time. Shannon's heart was a mess and much of the time he spent doubting his own salvation.

In light of this, he and Pam continued going to church an hour away seeking truth. He said his desire to go to church was a spiritual indicator for him.

> *"It was the only thing that gave me any indication of the*
> *assurance of my salvation. I doubted it, but I knew on the*
> *Lord's Day where I was supposed to be."*

It was a long time before he found any resolve from his sin and guilt. The pastor of the church he was attending preached a sermon on divorce. The sermon was very harsh against divorce:

> *"That preacher convicted me, chewed me up, and spit me*
> *out. I felt terrible. I almost left."*

But at the end of the message, Shannon found rest for his soul.

> *"Then the pastor said, 'But if you're in this situation, you can't*
> *unscramble the egg. The only thing you can do is live from*
> *point A to point B when the Lord calls you home.'"*

Almost two decades later, Shannon still wrestles with his decisions but has found a solid marriage and real friendship with Pam. None of the members from First Baptist Rapid City speak to him two decades later. There is still bitterness and anger within his family, but there is mutual respect. Before his fall, Shannon showed signs of isolation, a broken marriage, and high expectations.

> *"I've never tried to justify anything. I fell, and great was the fall of it. For me to tell you that it still doesn't hurt that I fell, I'd be telling a lie. I don't dwell on it. Maybe I haven't paid the price God wants me to pay yet. But I paid a price."*

Today, Shannon seeks out those who have made mistakes and has a heart of compassion for them. His heart is still guarded from the events years ago, but he is still a man of great wisdom who is seen as a mentor to many in his current church.

Chapter 7

Dominic – The Breaking Point

Dominic left a secular career when he felt the call of God upon his life. He found success in both churches he pastored, but conflict arose at the second. He felt high expectations upon him, his marriage was struggling, and there was great stress and pressure. At one point, he reached out to some of his leadership about his burnout, but his cries fell upon deaf ears. Someone close to him heard him, however, and his ministry was changed forever.

Dominic had fought a battle against resistant church leadership for so long that he had become burned out and prayed about his situation continually.

> *"I got to a point where I was just emotionally beaten up. But there comes a point where no matter how much Scripture I claimed, I was just losing it."*

He was considering leaving the ministry for his previous secular work to get some relief for his broken soul. But Dominic knew that this was hardly an option.

> *"The more years you spend in ministry, the harder it is to leave the ministry because you've left the marketplace and the career you had before."*

He also knew that divorce wasn't an option. For a pastor to divorce was to commit career suicide. He reached out to his support staff at one point, hinting at his burnout, even giving them resources on pastoral stress. They didn't hear his clanging warning bell of coming ministry failure.

He knew when the moment came when he went from broken to vulnerable.

> *"I finally got to a point where I meant it when I said it, 'I just can't do this anymore.' I lost my drive. That opened the door."*

The ministry had kept him in a marriage that seemed more like a casual friendship but now the floodgates of temptation had opened to his heart. He wasn't looking for an affair or for companionship, but when it was offered, it was accepted. The path that led him to this point was fraught with similar circumstances of other fallen pastors.

Many pastors seem to follow a similar path to the ministry. They grow up in church, are in a dynamic youth group, receive God's call to ministry, attend seminary, then head into the ministry. Dominic's story, like a good number of fallen pastors, follows a different route. He was called to the ministry later in life after working in the secular field and having a family. His wife, Margie, had experienced the troubles of the American pastor firsthand because her father had served in the ministry. She was naturally timid at the prospect of being a pastor's wife. Dominic said:

> *"When we got married, she never really signed on to the whole ministry thing."*

After receiving his call, they discussed the idea of pursuing ministry. It was apparent that Margie was extremely resistant to the idea, but Dominic was very passionate about the idea. Eventually, she reluctantly conceded, but would never fully be pleased about being a minister's wife:

> *"I just don't think she liked the idea of being in the fishbowl."*

Dominic went back to college to finish his degree and graduated from seminary.

He immediately took a pastorate in a small church in their home state of Oregon in a large city. Dominic was a man driven by his passion for the church. The church grew rapidly, baptized many, and even added building projects. Dominic found most of his free time filled with visiting older members. The church was the perfect size for one pastor to handle, but he would often find himself worn out. There were high expectations on him within the church from the older members to visit, the younger members wanted a place for their children to grow and Dominic placed pressure on himself to perform at an even higher level each day.

> "They expect you to be the world's best preacher; this spiritual, knobby kneed prayer warrior, the loving guy to all the kids and teens, as well as visit all the seniors and the sick."

During this time, his marriage was still struggling. He would often come home overwhelmed and exhausted but his wife was still dissatisfied with the ministry life:

> "Pastoring is tough, at best. Even if you have the quintessential pastor's wife, it's still hard. If you don't have it, it's almost impossible."

Dominic never blamed his problems on his wife, knowing that there were many times he should have done something to fix them. He described his marriage as committed yet admitted that even though he knew his wife wasn't happy, he was doing what he wanted to do.

> "Over a long period of time my career in ministry became my drive to the exclusion to my relationship at home. My work in ministry became a substitute for my marriage relationship."

After ten years, his church began to grow stagnant. Dominic had bigger plans and aspirations in mind so he started sending resumes out to see if there were larger churches he could pastor. He wanted to be able to effect change on a larger level, to do bigger things and to have a staff. He wanted everything that most pastors want after serving at a small church for a long time. After a couple of years, he found a church that seemed promising. The new church was a larger church but in a smaller town. After the first week, he discovered that the new church wasn't all he hoped it would be.

When he arrived, he found a church struggling with serious internal conflict. There were a group of classic older members who wanted things to stay the same, a group of younger members who were fighting them who wanted change and a group of deacon leaders who wanted to maintain control and didn't want the pastor to make changes. However, Dominic knew that if this church was going to impact the community, change had to occur. He made decisions that were in the best interest of the church and added programs that stimulated growth. He baptized more than the church had baptized in over two decades. People were growing, learning and finding a church home. Through it all though, Dominic had to battle the older power group for power.

> *"I knew I had some support from people in the church, but I still had to face the dragon. Sometimes I felt like I was fighting the dragon myself."*

Worse problems arose when budget issues came to the fore during a building program. He felt as if every financial issue was being put under a microscope. All of this conflict forced Dominic, a man who typically brought people together, to become a more aggressive personality at times. Through all of this conflict, he made headway and felt as if the church was finally turning the corner toward real growth and kingdom change. However, it had finally taken its toll on Dominic. He had reached a breaking point.

Sandra was a member of the church who was experiencing emotional issues of her own. There wasn't an overt sexual approach on either of their parts. A harmless friendship began and Sandra seemed to understand Dominic. She listened to him, took time for him, and encouraged him. Someone was finally listening to his struggles and understood his heart. An emotional relationship grew quickly which eventually led to a physical one. The relationship didn't last long before it was discovered and passed on to the deacon body. The response was quick and intense.

> *"I was asked to leave immediately. I was told to never step back in the pulpit."*

Margie left him immediately and he packed his belongings and moved in with an old friend in another town. His family was angry with his sin and most of his friends rejected him. He found work at a gas station as an attendant and tried to work on getting back into his old career. Sandra was out of his life very soon after his fall and he would never hear from her again.

Despite the horrible circumstances that followed his fall, Dominic felt a relief to be out of the ministry. He described it as a "huge weight." The ministry provides many ministers with stress, depression and anxiety, and Dominic was no exception.

> "It was terrific to be out. I didn't have to worry about the phone ringing at two in the morning for a funeral or illness, or deacon's meetings, or what attendance was going to be – I didn't have to worry about all these things that plague our souls in the ministry."

Dominic realized that the expectations placed on the pastor were high and should have been high. However, many of those expectations were unrealistic.

> "We live in a world where we have to be careful what we say and who we say it to, where we go, who we go with and how we're seen, how we're dressed – all of that is a pressure cooker for a lot of pastors. You're on duty 24/7."

After falling, Dominic was able to reflect on how the ministry impacted his personality.

> "When people ask me now what I used to do I hardly ever mention that I was a pastor."

He finds his new life less stressful than his previous one:

> "Pastors are subject to the same pressures and problems as anyone else, maybe even greater than others. You're just walking on eggshells all the time and you get pretty good at it."

Two years after his fall, Dominic met Cynthia, a woman who was going through trials of her own. Through this new relationship, he found peace and healing. They married and built a new and lasting relationship. He began to restore spiritually and anew with God. He also was able to reconcile with some of his former deacons through a series of letters. He knew the risk before he fell, but knows it even better now.

"Pastoring is like no other profession, even the president of the United States. Once you go down that road, it's almost impossible to come back. Once you wear that scarlet letter, you're branded."

Dominic became broken through a series of events in his life. He had serious communication issues with his wife, with whom he never agreed with on ministry goals and aspirations. He had extremely high expectations placed upon him by churches, which he internalized and was resisted by a conflicted church. When he reached his breaking point, he found no help but realized he was isolated from anyone who could give him help.

Chapter 8

Lance – Burned Out On People-Pleasing

Lance had done everything right, or so he thought. He had gone to a conservative seminary, found a wife whose values matched his, raised his children the right way, loved two congregations through music and teaching, yet his life was now in shambles. It didn't happen overnight, but it also didn't happen without warning.

His Christian life had been spent working out his salvation to please God and others. Serving the church was his first love and every moment was spent loving the church and the people within it. His love for music and ministry was great, but so were the stressors that went with them. His fall came quickly and the fallout was harsh. He described the first three months after his fall as his "own personal 9/11."

> *"Everything I was and everything people thought I was, was gone."*

His father, who had always loved and held him in high regard, left him a voicemail, which basically disowned him. After an email had been intercepted and turned into the leadership, the church from which he fell dismissed him quickly.

> *"They threw us away like garbage."*

He was told to resign immediately, hand in his keys and leave the premises.

> *"That was pretty hardcore stuff when it was all you ever wanted and all you ever knew."*

Lance grew up in a conservative, fundamentalist Baptist church with extremely rigid ideas about faith and practice. He described a theology where the sinner was saved by grace, but after salvation, sanctification was born by good works and keeping external laws of purity. His passion for God was sparked early as he was leading worship as early as middle school and preaching in high school. His works theology was buffered by his people-pleasing personality where he desired the approval of others on a regular basis.

From high school, he and his high school sweetheart, Stephanie, left for a conservative Bible college where he planned to study for the ministry. Lance and Stephanie had grown up together in the faith, always at church when the doors were opened, and had a strong fundamentalist Baptist upbringing. He was filling the normative plan for many evangelical youths. Two weeks after graduation, he and Stephanie were married.

> *"I had never really dated anyone else. People in our faith were expected to go to college, get married, find a job and start a family."*

Lance and Stephanie experienced great success in a couple of different churches after college and Lance found that he was able to branch out in his faith and appreciate more eclectic flavors than he had learned in his fundamentalist upbringing. His wife Stephanie, however, would always remain more comfortable with the conservative flavor of their youth. Lance's change of viewpoint in his religion compounded the communication issues that already existed between them.

> *"Communication was impossible for her, but I was the one who really changed the deal. We were moving in different spiritual directions. I learned early on in my marriage that I couldn't really speak my mind and that she was always right. And being a pleaser, that's the kind of thing you tuck away and you use as a survival tool on the journey."*

They had two children together during their early years in the ministry, but he described a lack of intimacy throughout their marriage.

*"Our marriage was a great business partnership. I was the
CEO, I was the visionary, I was providing for us that way.
She was taking care of the books, she was the CFO. We were
managing our little staff of children there the best we could.
We were like the All-American evangelical dream. But we
never had a relationship. The emotional connectivity and
intimacy part of our marriage was nonexistent. We had a
loveless marriage. I felt dirty because I was in need of sex
and had to somehow find the right moment to make sure
everything was right to even think about approaching her
so I could just, not emotionally connect or enjoy an intimate
experience, but to physically relieve myself. That will make
someone feel pretty low. And me being a preacher, I just
tried to make it work. But I just ended up pouring myself into
the ministry."*

While at his first church, he worked on a long-distance education seminary
degree. Several times a year, he had to travel hundreds of miles for classes.
On one occasion, he fell into the temptation of online pornography and
charged it to his credit card. His wife read the bill and tracked it down and
confronted him with his transgression. They had a long talk when he got
home from his seminary classes.

*"That was the first moment I knew I was weak, both in my
marriage and ministry."*

He pastored his first church for several years and wanted to leave, but
Stephanie did not want to leave the church, which caused him greater
heartache. Eventually, she reluctantly gave him permission to seek other
opportunities. He soon received a call to work as music minister at a church
in Hawaii. The church was progressive and seeker-sensitive. While he was
there, it grew from 150 to over 2,000 in a seven-year period. He poured his
time, passion and all his energy into the ministry, causing great pressure.

*"I don't think I placed pressure on myself, I was addicted
to it. It didn't feel like pressure to me. My body wasn't
accumulating it as pressure. It was a rush. It made me feel
successful. It was what I wanted. It was kind of an escape.*

It kept me distracted from trying to ask questions like, 'Why when I'm at home do I find myself in the garage smoking cigars and no one wants to come out and be around me? Where is all this anger coming from?' Those weren't the questions I started to ask until everything exploded."

The pressure took its toll and Lance came to a place of bitterness, desiring to move on.

"I was burned out but I didn't even know it. I really hated people all the time. That's a good sign you need to get checked out as a pastor."

The pastor at that church left and he stepped in as an interim, which caused even more stress. He served as the "unspoken" senior pastor for a period of three years before he decided he needed to move on.

"I didn't want to do anything but worship and worship arts. I had become the pastor, was teaching and preaching regularly, marrying and burying."

He began to actively search for another church and found one in the area. He and his wife found a church across the island that was expanding their building to suit their membership near 2,000. He enjoyed his new job and was able to work freely as worship pastor. His focus was still primarily on his ministry and not on his troubled marriage. His desire to please people continued to transform as he ministered:

"The more I saw I was getting out of what I was doing, the more I enjoyed it and the better I became at it. I have this theory that there's this evolutionary thing that happens to a person that we develop skill sets and abilities that foster our need to be approved."

Lance loved his new church and felt connected to the ministry in a whole new way. On staff was Kari, a woman he worked side by side with daily.

"We were really striding as a team. We had about a hundred staff members and we were just really hitting a home run as far as what the church was asking for. We were ramping

> *up and recruiting and getting ready to move into the new*
> *auditorium the church was building. I think being in charge,*
> *being the boss was something I was really jazzed by. I wasn't*
> *necessarily doing counseling or teaching, but I was free to*
> *do my thing."*

During the first year, they formed a solid friendship that was based on common interests and ministry goals.

> *"She and I worked well together. Neither of us really*
> *understood the places of our marriage at the time. A little*
> *over a year after I got there, it was obvious that it was more*
> *than just a friendship.*

With all the responsibilities, Lance was feeling stress again, but didn't realize it. The stress this time was positive stress. Their relationship began to evolve into an emotional relationship and both knew that what lay on the horizon. During a conference they both attended, they both realized the consequences of their future actions.

> *"It was at that point that we tried to say, 'We need to stop this,*
> *we need some help,' but it was too late. It was impossible."*

Two months after their emotional relationship began, they began a physical relationship.

> *"A month or two later we had a physical connection. Our*
> *relationship was everything an affair is – thrilling, there was*
> *physical attraction, and sex, because I had been oppressed*
> *for so long."*

Their relationship was soon discovered, and they were both dismissed from the church. Lance still has trouble recalling the months that followed.

> *"It blew up. Those first three months it's even hard for me to*
> *recall a lot of detail. We were both obviously at the bottom."*

The church made no move toward reconciliation or counseling, but simply sent Lance and Kari out the back door.

> *"The senior pastor never once picked up the phone and*
> *called me or pulled me into his office and said, 'What are you*

doing? What's going on?' It was, 'We accept your resignation.
We'll take your keys and goodbye.' And that was it."

After being dismissed from the church, both Kari and Lance worked on their respective marriages through counseling, but they felt they were irreconcilable.

> *"In my marriage at the time, I was told I needed to be something I really wasn't. I was saying through counseling, 'This is what I think, feel, believe and am asking for,' and I was told, 'No, that's not acceptable.'"*

After the divorces, Kari and Lance began to see each other. Lance described their relationship as "on again, off again" and they sought counseling as well. Both were still dealing with the emotional fallout after the fall and struggled to find themselves in the midst of it. However, through it all, they found support and peace.

> *"We got to the end of it all and discovered after so much hardship we still had a deep affinity for one another."*

After restoring themselves, they still had a deep angst toward the church in general. They were fortunate to connect to a church. After years of stress before the fall and a lack of restoration after, they found a church who loved them for who they were – broken people.

> *"That church really restored our faith in the institution of the church for us by investing in us as people. They approached us with a Christ-like attitude. They were interested in us as people. Instead of 'what skill set do you have and what can you do for us,' they said, 'we want you to come alongside you for your sake and for our sake.'"*

The church also sent Lance and Kari to an intensive ministry restoration center in Oahu for several weeks to heal. Together, they grew together and found peace and restoration as a Christian couple.

> *"This woman who so many have viewed as a Jezebel is now my best friend and I experience love with her like I never could have possibly known."*

In the time after his fall, Lance has had both positive and negative experiences with those in his former church.

> *"99% of the people we run into out in public have embraced us. They say, 'Hey, how are you, we miss you.' It's been very sincere. The leadership on the other hand is different. One leader reached out to me some time later and had lunch with me and tried to talk me into repenting. For him, that meant I had to forsake Kari, apologize to the church, my family and everyone else. I requested audience with the pastor and leadership and I went in and apologized and they dutifully accepted that but I never heard a peep from any of them again."*

Lance strives to move on daily, seeking Christ and serving him, attempting to put the past behind and live for the future. The hurt still exists in his heart, but over time, perspective has given him a good outlook where he is able to be patient with those in his past.

> *"The hurt comes from not the people, because I think the people I served and were under my ministry realized that I am human and I will make mistakes. Some of them still don't understand why I got divorced. But for the most part, people have been gracious but the staff has not been."*

Lance described two other situations in the church that occurred since he left. Two other staff members were discovered in affairs and were dismissed in the same manner in which he was. Such repeat problems within the church culture might strike the church to ask where the core of the problem lies.

> *"I'm wondering, are people going to say, 'What's happening?'"*

When asked how he thought the church leadership should have handled the situation, Lance replied:

> *"I would have liked to see the leadership be more proactive. To even find out what restoration was."*

He then referenced Galatians 6:1 as a model for restoration.

> *"Brothers, when one of you is overtaken in a fault, you who are spiritual, restore such a one in a spirit of meekness, considering yourself, lest you also be tempted."*

Lance reflected on thinking about dwelling on the past and moving too far into the future:

> *"The past can be slavery and the future can be idolatry. Don't look back, don't look too far forward or you'll miss what's happening right now where the kingdom and spirit are."*

Lance and Kari are still moving toward healing in their relationship with the church. They both understand the depth of their sin and yet appreciate God's redemptive work in their life. Before his fall, Lance experienced high expectations from his church, but much of his expectations were self-imposed. Many of his expectations were a result of his own people pleasing personality and his focusing his energy away from his marriage problems and into his ministry work. Lance found comfort close by at work in a sympathetic partner who was also broken. Lance sums up his story this way:

> *"I'm not ashamed of my story because God wouldn't have forged something in me without it."*

Chapter 9

Vincent – Addicted To Appreciation

Vincent had been living with high expectations from his Methodist counterparts for some time. The weight of the stress was strong and he was in constant desperation for acceptance and appreciation. It had created in him a need for increasing acceptance and he had looked elsewhere. He had crossed the line months before and had been discovered. The staff members in Vincent's church discovered his adultery. Instead of confronting him, they went directly to the district superintendent. Not every fallen pastor's story ends in divorce. Many are able to find reconciliation with their wives through those who are willing to walk with them.

Vincent immediately went to his wife, Vivian and told her. He then told his leadership committee and confessed. The district superintendent summoned him and Vivian into a meeting where he was ordered to confess. He described it as a "brutal interrogation" for two hours in the presence of his wife. The superintendent and other leaders wanted to know details of the affair. Methodist ministers have certain rights that apply to hearings and he was not told of his rights at that time.

"I was led to believe I was beyond repair and worthless."

Despite being betrayed and the depths of her hurt, Vivian had decided to stand by her husband. Vivian spoke up at one point and said, "You know, Vincent is a gifted pastor." During that meeting, he begged them for help. They told him he needed to ask his family physician for a referral to a psychiatrist because he was beyond their help. Vincent said:

> *"It was like they had never experienced anyone committing adultery."*

At this moment, it seemed as if the denominational leadership were trying to destroy him instead of restore him. Over the next few weeks, this type of treatment would continue in an attempt to make Vincent surrender his orders. He was made to feel like the worst sort of wretch imaginable.

> *"Adultery is the one unforgivable sin in the United Methodist Church as a pastor. It's okay to be gay, it's okay to be an alcoholic, it's okay to have a divorce, but it's not okay to commit adultery and stay with your wife."*

Vincent had found his niche in Toledo. His first appointment out of the Methodist seminary was to a church of 400. In 20 years, he had taken the church through a large building project and had a steady attendance of 900. The church and community loved him so much, they often begged the district superintendent not to reassign him to another city.

The Methodist denomination bragged on him and his success, holding him up as a blueprint for others to follow. Other pastors often pointed to his church as a model for what other churches in the state should be doing. In his own heart, he wanted to be successful in the denomination and knew the expectations were great.

> *"I felt there was a huge pedestal and I internalized a lot of expectations about being a perfect pastor and having a perfect organization."*

The problem with such expectations for Vincent was that he was emotionally needy. He was in constant need of affirmation and appreciation and often felt like he wasn't getting enough, whether at home, church or from the denomination. He and his wife had grown distant in the previous years and had been living individual lives. He explained his relationship to the appreciation he so desperately craved:

> *"It's like a drug addiction. There is some appreciation there. But it wasn't enough. It's like taking heroin. You need more and more and more. The insecurity comes back more strongly each time."*

He had been placed on a pedestal by his church and denomination and knew he wasn't worthy of such praise, but still allowed himself to be seen in that way. Despite the praise from the denomination and local office, he wasn't close to any of them and was isolated in his role as pastor. He enjoyed the positive attention, even craving it, but always needed more, but it created a double-edged sword of idolization and self-doubt:

> *"Part of the issue is isolation and being on a pedestal and needing to be on the pedestal and needing affirmation. The more successful it was, the more self-doubt I would have."*

Vincent, like many other broken ministers before, began to get close to a co-worker. She offered so much of what he needed at the time. She had a wonderful personality, was emotionally needy herself, and he felt he could share anything with her. She offered him a deep adoration he had been seeking for a long time and felt he had not been receiving in his marriage.

> *"One of the things the person I got involved with offered was this kind of adoration. My counselor told me later, 'the higher you are, the longer the shadow you cast.'"*

Their relationship began with shared time in prayer and spiritual matters. It progressed to an emotional relationship then crossed the forbidden boundary into the physical.

Vincent took full responsibility for his sin and after the initial meeting with the leadership, he and Vivian sought counseling and restoration. During that time, the denomination still sought the surrender of his orders. He finally surrendered them and went to work as an insurance salesman. He had been shamed by his sin, the denomination turned their back on him and he was now the disgrace of the community. He had been in the denomination in Toledo for over 20 years, had over 400 colleagues and after his fall, yet he heard from only one active pastor who gave him words of support.

Through time and counseling, Vincent found redemption and solace.

> *"When we entered therapy, I had a good perspective. I realized I was not beyond repair. Part of the reconciliation*

*between me and my wife was we realized how we had
become distant and led individual lives."*

Removal gave him ample time to reflect upon his own experience. He still
had many in his old church who loved him deeply and kept in contact with
him. However, the denominational authorities still regarded him as a threat
and never reconciled with him.

*"The organizational parts of the church can't really deal
with redemption. It can only deal with trying to cut out the
cancer."*

Vincent discovered that many of his former church members were leaving
their church. Their reasons for quitting their former church varied. Some
were disillusioned because of his adultery, some did not care for how the
denomination had treated him and some felt that if the church couldn't
forgive, they couldn't be forgiven either. Some of the members decided
to start their own non-denominational church and they invited Vincent to
be their pastor. After much prayer and self-searching, Vincent accepted. He
had come to a place where he realized his call in Christ was greater than
something a denomination could give.

*"I realized that even though I was ordained by a
denomination, it wasn't the denomination that called me,
it was Christ that called me. Christ did not rescind the call."*

Vincent has changed from his first pastoral experience. Going through
such an experience of brokenness has made him realize his limitations.

*"I became very transparent as their new pastor. I wasn't
seeking to create a successful organization this time. I don't
wish to be fed by organizational successes."*

His very character has changed as well as his impetus for doing ministry.

*"I am open to the possibility of my ego going awry. I'm a
broken person who does ministry."*

Vincent no longer chases ministry. It is ministry that comes to him. Before,
he pursued the higher goals and successes that a life of denominationalism
offered, but now, as a broken and wounded minister, he is able to be

transparent before his congregation. He can now embrace the man he has become.

> *"I know I have shadows and I can acknowledge, embrace, and ride into those shadows. I am no longer interested in presenting myself."*

Chapter 10

Gary – Escape From Reality

It was such a beautiful scene from the third story balcony of the 2,000-member Grand View Baptist Church just outside New Orleans. Senior Pastor, Bro. Gary Preston used to brag to visiting pastors how one could see the ocean on one side and the city on the other. The job had been everything he had ever wanted. It had a large membership, lots of programs and a huge outreach. But pressure had come with it. High expectations were coupled with increased separation from his wife, Elizabeth.

Now, as he stood here with his old friend Brad from seminary, he only had one thought. "Jump." A three story fall should kill him quickly. Put him out of his misery. And right now, he had what it took to do it.

He wanted life to end. It seemed like it was all ending at this moment anyway. He had just told Brad everything. He had told him how he had been carrying on with his wife's best friend Amy for four months. The relationship had started innocently enough but got carried away. Gary explained to Brad that all he had really wanted was attention, acceptance and appreciation. He had explained to Brad that what he wanted was for him to hold him accountable. Brad, a pastor of a small church who had a questionable past before his conversion, didn't draw the same conclusion.

"You need to tell Elizabeth," Brad had said quickly, directly, and full of conviction.

"Excuse me? I can't tell my wife!" Gary had said, with all the weight of a pastor whose church was ten times the size of Brad's.

Brad didn't flinch. "Your conscious is too sensitive, Gary. You can't live with this. You're going to tell your wife."

Gary stared down at the parking lot below again. Thinking of his children, he snapped back to sanity, knowing what he had to do. He walked down the stairs and got into his car. It was Wednesday night and literally, all hell was about to break loose. "It hadn't always been like this," he thought. "How did I get here?"

Years ago, Gary had always dreamt of having a large church with many resources. He had always had a big presence in the pulpit and stood out among his peers in seminary. He pastored a church out of seminary with 200 members for a few years when Great View came calling. He knew Great View Baptist was the church of his dreams when he first laid eyes on their sanctuary. His sermons were televised and the church loved his charisma and personality. The two were a match made in heaven. Reflecting back, Gary wonders if ministry in the church had not become an idol for him:

> "My dream should have been a person and not a church or ministry." He reflected upon Philippians 3:10, "That I might know [Christ] and the power of His resurrection."

Gary's drive for the ministry was overpowering. He had a desire to do better than the previous pastor. This meant being present for every meeting, activity and event on the calendar. He would work every day of the week from early in the morning to late at night.

> "It was all rooted in the sin of fearing man. I wanted to be impressive, to be bigger than life, to do better than anyone had ever done before."

He did feel like there were great expectations placed upon him by his church, but they could not be any greater than the expectations he placed upon himself. At the base of it all, Gary felt very insecure. His insecurity pushed him even harder to perform at higher levels.

Not surprisingly, this drive placed a great deal of tension between him and his wife Elizabeth. His desire for the church made Elizabeth feel less desired emotionally, spiritually, and physically. Concurrently, he felt less desired by Elizabeth. However, Gary was so consumed with church and doing the work of the church that he failed to notice or care about the failure of his marriage. Often in such situations, pastors feel the work of church trumps the problems of their marriage, or they feel that their wives should be more understanding of them since they are doing ministry work.

Two crisis points developed that began to push Gary over the edge. The first was when his mother fell ill and died. She had been his biggest supporter in life. Gary's mom was his largest source of prayer, encouragement and affirmation. Her death would linger with Gary for a long time and he never found anything to fill the hole that she left in his heart. Secondly, a staff member at church was failing to do his job. One of the worship leaders had been slacking in his work and complaining about his pay. The staff member resigned amidst a small amount of complaining and conflict.

During this time, Elizabeth encouraged Gary to start a friendship with a couple in the church, Mike and Tina. Gary felt as if he didn't have enough time to start a friendship, didn't want to get close to anyone in the church, and frankly shared later:

> *"I didn't even care for them."*

Elizabeth insisted and they began to hang out at Mike and Tina's house after church in the evening. At first, everyone would joke how Gary would look at his watch when he wanted to leave. As the visits continued, Gary stopped.

Gary wanted to stay because he had developed an attraction for Tina. She was giving Gary a lot of attention and affirmation that he had been starving for, but Gary was directly unaware of it:

> *"I wasn't conscious of it at the time, if that makes sense."*

Tina was laughing at his jokes, listening intently to all of his comments, telling him how wonderful his sermons were and explaining to him how much she had grown spiritually because of him. He said:

> *"I found myself going to their house to be around her. I was talking to her instead of talking to him and going to visit so I could see her and not him."*

The church had an annual hayride with field events in which prizes were given. It was the one time each year where Gary let his hair down a little. Mike, Tina and Elizabeth were on his team and they were supposed to pair up with their spouses for a relay event called, "The Apple Race." Each couple was supposed to bite into an apple at the same time and carry it thirty yards. Gary and Elizabeth had been quarreling all day, so Elizabeth had no interest in the games.

"Come on, Elizabeth, are you going to do this with me or what?" Gary said.

"No, I really don't feel like it," Elizabeth said.

"How about you, Tina? You want to do The Apple Race with me?" it was an impulsive question, and he blurted it out. It hung there, but he couldn't take it back.

Tina looked at Elizabeth, eyebrows raised, "Do you mind?"

"Go for it," Tina said noncommittally.

They raced together, faces as close as they could possibly be. They hung out the rest of the night and Mike and Elizabeth didn't seem to care. They even began to give one another celebratory hugs after winning races. She began to embrace him more fully each time and he noticed. He thought:

> "This isn't what I think it is. She's a good girl. She loves her husband and her kids, so this is okay."

That day, a few people casually mentioned his contact with Tina.

The next day, he received a call from Tina, which caused him some level of excitement. She had called about something unimportant, but she asked a question that created a turning point for him: "Did anyone else say anything about our apple race?"

He was slightly stunned, but something in him made him play along, "No, but I hope it wasn't too much for you." That comment, that day, was the moment something was officially unleashed in him.

That Friday, Gary and Elizabeth visited Tina and Mike for dinner. When they arrived, Tina was wearing a low-cut top that he had never seen her wear. All night, she seemed to be trying to get Gary's attention. Toward evening's end, they found themselves alone on the patio when Mike and Elizabeth walked to the other end of the property to check on the kids. Gary moved his foot and it brushed up against Tina's. She smiled and began to return the favor. There was an unspoken conversation occurring that was confusing to Gary but he was enjoying the positive attention.

Finally, they both stood up. She brushed up against him and Gary finally said, "What in the world are we doing?"

Tina stepped back, surprised, putting her head down, embarrassed.

"What?" Gary said confused.

"I feel like I just got caught," she said still looking down.

"What are you talking about? What are we doing? What is going on here?" he asked trying to put the pieces together.

"I think we're attracted to each other," she said.

"Well, Tina, I can't do this, I'm a pastor!" he said blurting out his words forcefully and almost pridefully.

She was almost offended, "Well, I'm a Sunday School teacher!"

He paused for a moment, looking in her eyes, "Where do you think this is going to lead?"

"I figured something might happen," she said, then smiled at him.

He couldn't help but return the smile. They knew their spouses would be a while with the children. They took a while to talk and flirt before they returned. Gary was still careful to not cross any lines. He was soaking up the attention he was receiving and Tina seemed to enjoy giving it to him. At this point, it all seemed harmless. Gary said about it later:

> "It's the smiles, the innocent touches, the flirting, the affirmation, the winks. I even used to think, 'I'll get close to the fire but I won't get burned.' Proverbs 6:27 says, 'Can a man carry fire next to his chest and his clothes not be burned?'"

On Monday, he was in a staff meeting and received an email from Tina. She told him that she was going to be in the area and wanted to know when would be the best time for her to see him. He gave her a time. She showed up after working out and he did something he had never done before – he closed his office door behind her. They began to talk about the state of their relationship, their feelings and how they were struggling with temptation.

She then said, "I'd like to kiss you."

"I'm not going to initiate anything," Gary replied. Not a firm answer, but maybe it would exonerate him if anything happened or if a staff member walked in.

She crawled into his lap and kissed him. He didn't resist. In fact, he fully participated. Over the next thirty minutes, passion was shared and they came close to consummating their relationship. She left the office first and he left an hour later with a burden of guilt. She set up two secret email accounts for them that night so they could exchange messages without discovery. They began to discuss the possibility of getting a hotel room. He wasn't sure about it, but after two days of considering it, he agreed.

He described the feeling before the encounter as "numb." After it happened, he said he told himself, "I'm not going to do this anymore." Guilt overwhelmed him as he realized what he had done.

> *"But then you get low, feel depressed and tell yourself 'we're the only ones who will know,' and you do it again."*

Gary stated that leads to a sort of moral crumbling.

> *"You find yourself doing it again and again and you're like, 'Who cares? What's it matter now?'"*

Their secret relationship went on for three months. Gary stated that Mike had suspicions right away. At one point, Mike approached him about it, but he denied it. Gary kept preaching, kept the façade of his marriage and ministry together while he felt he was falling deeply for Tina.

> *"You feel like you're in love. You're living in a fantasy world with no responsibility."*

However, the strain became more than he could bear.

One Wednesday afternoon, he came home to find Tina helping Elizabeth organize the house. When Elizabeth wasn't in the room, they flirted and he returned to work. His soul had been stirred by seeing Elizabeth and Tina together at his home. His mind, heart and spirit were beginning to unravel. Tina called him at work and something had come over him.

"What are we doing? How are we going to get out of this?" he asked her as he began to cry. He realized she was the only one he could confide in.

"Gary, you need to talk to someone you can trust about this. You're losing it," she suggested.

That's when Gary turned to Brad, a seminary friend with a rough past and whom he was sure would keep his secret. Yet Brad was now urging him to reveal everything and he knew it would at least cost him his ministry, but it might cost him his marriage. Gary knew Brad was right. He began to make his way down the interior stairs. He was looking for Steve, one of his associate pastors. He told Steve the brief account of his sin. Steve hugged him and told him he had suspected it for a while. Gary told him to pull the sermons from the local television station to avoid embarrassment when the news came out.

By the time he had finished, Elizabeth was home and his heart was sick. He decided on the direct approach. Before talking to her, he texted Tina, "I'm about to tell my wife." He found Elizabeth in the living room on the couch relaxed. It would be the last time she would be relaxed for a long time.

"Elizabeth, I've been having an affair with Tina for three months. We've had sex ten times," he said bluntly, looking her in the eyes.

"Oh, you're crazy," she said, barely looking up from what she was doing.

"I'm serious," he said firmly.

He said of that moment:

> "I thought if I just told her right there it would just end it all
> and she'd just say 'get out' and I could get a new start."

It took her a moment, but the rage built in her. She was easily a foot shorter than him, but she ran to him screaming, punching and full of emotions Gary had never witnessed in her.

The next 24 hours turned into a back and forth between the two couples. Deacons and church leaders were showing up at Gary's house offering to walk them through their situation. Gary drove to see Tina at a hotel room she had gotten after Mike had kicked her out. He had to talk to her about their relationship. Gary knew his life was rapidly falling apart, that he had a family to take care of and that reality had finally found him.

He was torn at that moment but knew what he had to say and do. He was torn because they had a meaningful relationship. Reflecting on it he said:

> "The sin of adultery messes you up like no other sin. You become so connected to that person you feel responsible for them and it's hard to break that connection. It becomes addictive."

"Go back to your husband, Tina," he said to her.

She started to scream at him, "I was ready to leave everything for you!" Gary was torn but knew he had church leaders holding him accountable for his actions. He left her there, never to see her again.

The next night, he and Elizabeth met with the church administration, trustees and deacons and told them what he had done. He said, "I've had an affair. I'm no longer worthy to be your pastor." Reactions were mixed among the group. Some were so hurt they left. Some embraced him and his wife with great emotion. Others shook their head and refused to have anything to do with them. Some suggested to him that he stay, but he knew that wasn't an option. The next day, he was asked by church leadership to sign a resignation letter. Much of the church leadership was harsh in their treatment of him, due to their hurt. He said:

> "The church really didn't know how to handle it. They were clueless."

He was given the opportunity to write out a letter of resignation that was read before the church the following Sunday. Some of the congregation came to his home after the service and told him they loved him. One of his church members who owned a large business offered him work as an entry-level electrician which he readily accepted. It wasn't close to the money he was making as a mega-church pastor, but it was work nonetheless.

"I would describe the next year as a year of terrible drought and emotional devastation."

His marriage was in shambles and his spiritual life was in disarray. Thankfully, he had many great men of God who surrounded him and offered him and his wife support. It was a long process of recovery. He discovered that he had much pride in the beginning, but submitted to counseling and worked with them. It was a time of searching and terrible pain for him.

"You tell people that and they say, 'Well, you made your bed, so you go lie in it.' But it's still painful."

After his fall, he did not have many fellow pastors who reached out to him, even while he was going through his restoration process.

"I think people fear that if they affirm you after your sin, they're affirming your sin. Somehow it has to be communicated that it's possible to say that what you did is horrible, what you did is grievous, but I love you and I want to see you do well and I want to see God's grace upon you."

Gary is a pastor who knows of the hurt after a fall. Fallen pastors are in need of love like any Christian who commits a major sin. However, fallen pastors are often seen as an albatross no one wants to approach:

"I heard about a pastor who committed adultery in August then killed himself in December. I wondered, 'Did anyone reach out to him? Did anyone love him? Did anyone seek to restore him?' It brought back so many memories of when I wanted to die."

A year after his restoration process, Gary received a call from the chair of a pulpit search committee in Baton Rouge. They knew of his story and his fall and asked him and Elizabeth to meet with them. After meeting, they were excited about his restoration and invited him to preach and share his testimony. The church received his testimony with grace and called him to pastor:

"I didn't know if I'd ever be in ministry again. I didn't know if anyone would have me."

Years after his fall, Gary and Elizabeth had learned much about forgiveness. Elizabeth, who went through a long process of grief and sorrow over Gary's sin, opened her heart to him and showed grace to him. She also forgave Tina for her sin as well, giving Elizabeth spiritual and emotional freedom again. The process was not easy, but made them a couple ready for ministry again – more ready than they were the first time.

Gary knows he is a different man after being broken. Before his fall, he was judgmental and condemnatory on sin. Now, he considers himself more transparent.

> *"I know what shame is. I know it's not fun. I still confront but I try to love and restore."*

Chapter 11

Denny – The Fallen Pioneer

Denny had broken barriers that few had broken before. He had done things decades before anyone had ever dreamed of trying them. Unfortunately, that type of change raised eyebrows among his contemporaries. Denny craved acceptance with people. It was one of the things that drove him most. He began to be frowned upon by his state convention and this led to feelings of rejection. Denny knew he was wrong to do it, but the door had been opened to a dangerous path.

It was the third time the Alabama Baptist Convention had threatened to kick Brother Denny's church out of the state convention. He waited with a mix of anxiety, trepidation and angst as the board deliberated his church's fate. As he sat in the foyer of the hotel where the annual convention was held, he began to reflect on his efforts as a pastor at a university campus church.

The year was 1982 and as Denny put it, the battle in Southern Baptist circles was about "who believed the Bible the most." His church had been planted there to reach the college students and the people in the area and he had been given permission to use whatever means possible. He hadn't really wanted to be a pastor, but he felt called by God. He also had other aspirations to be a motivational speaker. He had reluctantly accepted the position, and over the next ten years the church exploded to 400.

And then someone in the church nominated a woman to be deacon and he didn't oppose it, so he was labeled a liberal. The state board called him about his non-opposition to women deacons but narrowly allowed him to stay. When they found out he didn't use a pulpit, he was again threatened. Denny joked:

> *"I thought, what's the best way to communicate on a college campus? I was sitting on a barstool before it was popular."*

The removal of the pulpit once again branded him as a liberal.

The state board called him a third time when his church sponsored a "hoedown" during the week. They asked for an account. The hoedown had been the church's idea for an outreach opportunity and he had supported it. He answered, "I don't know if you've ever seen a hoedown, but I don't see where it gets anyone in trouble. Besides, we shared the gospel, baptized six and I thought we were a Baptist church and had the right to make our own decisions." Once again, the state board backed down.

The constant questioning of his leadership by the state was revealing his weakness – his need of acceptance. Deep down, Denny had a need to be accepted:

> *"It's a strength and a weakness of mine."*

His church loved him for who he was. He was a dynamic leader who was able to counsel, lead, preach and win souls to Christ, yet he was often rejected by his peers for taking risks, which led to an emotional crisis. This was coupled with trouble at home involving unresolved anger with his wife, who he often had difficulty communicating with:

> *"That was the thing that put me under and cost me and that I'm totally responsible for. She was a good person."*

As a driven pastor and leader, he threw himself into his work even more trying to prove himself and find acceptance.

Denny tried to get out of the pastorate at one point to pursue his dream of motivational speaking. He told the church he was going to leave within a year, but they persuaded him to stay on for an additional two years to start a large outreach program. His compassion for the church made him reconsider even though he wasn't sure he had it in him.

> *"You get that noble feeling and begin to believe them when they say, 'We can't do it without you.'"*

He felt tired and burdened by the ministry but felt obligated by the people under his care. His duty to the many outweighed his own dreams and ambitions.

During those two years as the state convention continued their pressure, he felt further and further from his dream, and his relationship with his wife began to worsen. He felt desperately lost and each day the reality of who he wanted to be was becoming separated from who he really was. He knew he needed help, but he was alone in the world that had been created for him. His need of personal acceptance was screaming at him subconsciously.

> *"I don't know if I would have had an affair or not if I had felt accepted in the denomination, but I sure didn't feel like there was anyone I could go talk to."*

Denny found comfort with a woman his own age in the church. She was someone he "clicked with" and felt "accepted" by. It only lasted three months and stayed very quiet, successfully keeping it from the church and his wife. Despite the emotional acceptance, it was a time of intense shame and guilt. The moment he first crossed the line physically with her, he knew he was out of bounds and the moral weight of what he had done crushed him.

Even though he was able to hide it, he felt as if there was nowhere to hide.

> *"She knew, I knew, and God knew."*

Denny couldn't live with the guilt any longer. Denny cut off the relationship with this woman, resigned his position and left to take a job as a motivational speaker, hoping to leave his sin behind him. He was able to stay in the same town and work for a firm who willingly employed him.

Denny's sin was not concealed for long, however. Three months after he left the church, the woman he had committed adultery with shared the details of their relationship with a few of the deacons. An accountability group called him in for a meeting and demanded to know everything that occurred in detail. They had every detail of the affair correct and the woman had told them everything. He refused to confirm any specific accusations, but simply replied, "I'm guilty."

After five hours, the accountability group resolved to walk him through a restoration process and told him they would keep his transgression a secret. He felt confident of their confidentiality because he had counseled the majority of them through marriage and financial infidelity. He drove home and when he arrived, his wife knew every detail of his affair. The next day, she filed for divorce. There was no possibility of reconciliation and she left him immediately. The church leadership had turned on him.

> "It was like I died. There was no reaching out to me. I used to say we shoot our wounded, but we shoot them in the head."

Despite the fact that he was known statewide for winning people to Christ, there was hardly anyone who reached out to him.

> "I just found it amazing that no one from my church, absolutely no one called and no one checked with me."

Two individuals from outside his church did reach out to him. A Roman Catholic priest reached out to him as well as a local Fellowship of Christian Athletes leader. Both basically said to him, "Denny, we don't care what you've done. You're still Denny, nothing has changed. You're only finished if you think you're finished. But you're going to finish because God doesn't think you're finished or you'd be dead."

The first few months after Denny fell were filled with fear and loneliness. Usually a man of transparency and openness, he was guarded and confused. He began to see a counselor who helped him work through his deep emotional issues. He was very well known in his town and the scandal was the hot topic. Living in a town of over 300,000, he would walk into a public place and feel like everyone was talking about him. However, his counselor set him straight and said, "That's a pretty big ego you have, to think they care that much about you."

Through counseling, Denny began to understand the feelings of guilt and shame he possessed over the sin he had committed. While talking to his counselor, he also began to understand a greater good that God had for his life.

> "My sin had cost me. I'm sorry I had to go through that and I'm really sorry I hurt people, but it has caused me to go into

a deeper appreciation for God's forgiveness and walk with people who are trying to find forgiveness."

He had seen the view of his own sin up close and knew that he was vulnerable and weak. He also knew that he could help others once his own heart was healed.

Today, Denny is a successful motivational speaker whose message resonates with many. On the side, he listens to the stories of many broken people, including fallen pastors and those who have been affected by their falls. Like many fallen pastors, Denny's sin caused him to view his life and relationship to others differently and has changed the core of his message and ministry to others.

"I'm more sensitive in the little things of life now. I have a better perspective on life. A wholeness. God can take a tragedy that I didn't want to use for good and that just amazes me."

His heart for fallen pastors comes from an authentic desire to help and heal those who have been upon a similar path. He knows that his advice is only the beginning and they need a good counselor to help them along the path. Denny says to fallen pastors:

"Wherever you are, God still loves you."

Then he tells them what all fallen pastors need to hear, whether it comes from those they have hurt or a friend who is willing to stand by them in their restoration process:

"I don't necessarily have answers for you, but I will walk with you and try to find answers."

Chapter 12

Joe – Two Wrongs

Joe's fall is slightly different than the others. He had high expectations placed upon him as a minister and was placed upon a pedestal. However, the trigger that participated in his ultimate fall was a traumatic event. He was rejected quickly by his church leadership and found a very long road back to forgiveness.

Joe had a smile that was contagious and spread across the room when he entered. He had been pastoring for three years and had only been saved for five. He still had a strong passion for Christ that seemed unyielding to any external pressure. Seven years earlier, you would have found Joe and his wife Serena barhopping across St. Louis any night they could get free from their work. However, by the grace of God, a Pentecostal minister named Brother Alva had found Joe and witnessed to him. A transformation took place overnight that set Joe on the road to the pastorate.

Serena's salvation seemed sincere at the time, but she hadn't been as passionate as Joe. She went willingly into the ministry, but not as wide-eyed. To her, the parsonage was a nice arrangement and the pay and benefits were a welcome pleasantry from the blue-collar work either she or Joe had been used to. The people were nice to her so she settled in comfortably into their new home. She did, however, miss their days of recklessness and all her old friends were gone. Mike said:

> "She never really came into the identity of a pastor's wife or what it meant to be a believer."

Their new neighbors, Courtney and Mike were nice and Mike seemed to have a bit of a jaded past that was attractive to Serena. Joe became immersed in his training for ministry and he and Serena began to grow apart, though neither of them realized it.

During his rise, he realized that his mentor, Brother Alva, was the only authentic friend he had in ministry. There was no one he could confide in or share accountability with. He had not necessarily alienated people on purpose. His ministry was moving so fast and his training was progressing so quickly that he hardly had time to invest in personal relationships.

Joe accepted a call to a church and it became very successful under his charismatic leadership. He dove into every project with his giddy enthusiasm and passion for church growth. His zeal rubbed off on other members, which created high hopes for his church. The expectations were lofty upon him as a young pastor.

> *"I was the savior, if you will. They had me high up there, too high. I was to live above reproach, but they put me even above that. They had me up on a pedestal, almost in the place of an idol."*

Joe recognized that even though the expectations were high, he allowed them. Like many pastors, he enjoyed the attention and praise that was being lavished upon him.

> *"Ministers like that. We like the praise of people, but not understanding you'll die by the criticism. We deceive ourselves and place ourselves so high and begin to think we are untouchable."*

Despite the fact that Joe was doing so much good in his church and community, he had a false sense of security about himself.

Joe flourished as a pastor until his ministry came to an unexpected halt. Three years into his pastorate, Joe discovered that his wife, Serena had been engaged in a two-year affair with his neighbor, Mike. Courtney, Mike's wife broke the life-changing news. Joe was devastated.

> *"It was crushing when I found out."*

He knew it meant the end of his ministry career.

> *"I didn't seek help and I wasn't under accountability. The isolation took me over as soon as it happened."*

Joe confronted Serena immediately with her sin then told his mentor, but told no one else. Instead of taking a turn for redemption and forgiveness, his heart turned another direction – toward revenge. His mind and emotions spiraled out of control and his passions turned toward Courtney. They began to talk about how their spouses had sinned against them and their brief affair began. It only lasted a month. Joe said:

> *"I didn't walk in a long time of denial and I didn't try to cover it up. God didn't let me get away with anything."*

Mike had secretly videotaped Joe and Courtney's rendezvous and approached him with the evidence, but Joe already knew everything was about to come crashing down around him. He kept going to church as usual and preaching as if nothing had happened. On a Wednesday night, Brother Alva approached him with the videotape that Mike given him. Brother Alva demanded his resignation and then stood in front of his congregation and humiliated him and Courtney with his sins.

> *"Then he then met privately with me and scolded, judged, and condemned me in that meeting."*

Within a month, Joe had gone from rising star in the Pentecostal church to outcast. He moved to Chicago where he sat under the teaching of a well-known preacher for several years, seeking restoration of his faith. In that church, he found himself surrounded by men who were willing to help him find peace despite the pain within his heart.

> *"I came to a point where I said, 'Lord, I just want to be able to live without fear or guilt or frustration and I want to live inside a relationship with you again.'"*

Joe had found humility through his sin and pain, realizing that his pride had led him to such a fall. The ministry had been a way for him to help others, but it had also been the focus of his energy, not Christ. His misaligned passions and sin had brought him down, but showed him the need for a new heart.

> *"It showed me the state of the flesh and the pastor's heart, that we're all weak and we all have sinned and fall short of the glory of God whether we're in the pew or pulpit."*

During that process, he and Courtney found themselves pursuing a relationship toward one another. Both of their previous marriages had ended in divorce, so they sought out godly counsel on how to restore their lives and seek a right relationship together. It was a struggle, especially knowing that statistically, the vast majority of such relationships never survive.

> *"It took at least four years to get a strong foundation in our marriage to get to a place where the pain, guilt and shame wouldn't overwhelm us."*

Joe and Courtney were eventually able to find victory over these feelings and build a solid marriage.

Joe also began to feel that God wasn't finished with him in the ministry. However, his thoughts about the ministry had changed. He realized that before, he had been chasing after the ministry; but now, he needed to pursue Christ first. It was a seven-year journey under careful watch, but he was eventually restored to ministry within the Pentecostal church.

> *"For me, I was pursuing to get back into an intimate relationship with the Lord. There are so many men who want to be restored to ministry but they miss the whole point of being restored back to the Lord. It may never happen. The minister may never come back. But their relationship with the Lord is what fell before they fell."*

Joe knows that his fall and restoration show a transformation that God has done in his life. He is a different kind of pastor now than he was before his brokenness. Joe's heart had been broken by his sin and he was able to reflect upon the kind of person he had been and compared it to the type of person Christ wanted him to be.

"Before, I had a legalistic mindset counter to Scripture. Before my fall even the way I ministered was from a Pharisaical viewpoint. You don't see it when you're doing it until you need grace or mercy. There's a lot more compassion now."

Through years of restoration and preaching, Joe fills a need to minister to fallen pastors. He even feels the pain of the former sin from time to time and is able to walk with fallen pastors through that fresh experience.

"You can have 1,000 people pray over you but you get alone with your thoughts and the enemy's voice starts speaking to you and you get swept back into that pain and depression really fast."

Joe understood the plight of so many and opened a volunteer part time ministerial counseling service. Joe now sees his life as God's plan for him and Courtney.

"After seven years of restoration, the pain didn't affect us anymore. Eleven years and four children later, the ministry has a purpose that God has restored in our life and the dream is real."

Chapter 13

Josh – Rediscovering His First Love

Josh had seemingly done everything he could for his little church and for his wife. Despite their small size, expectations were high. He matched those expectations with greater output of his time. Struggles arose at home and Josh and his wife drifted apart. Josh began drifting away from the troubles of work and home and into a trap.

Josh remembers it for what it was.

> *"It was the biggest mistake of my life."*

He and his business partner, Matt, were driving home from a road trip to meet some clients. Josh was a bi-vocational pastor and had been busy with his investing business trying to make ends meet at home. Matt talked him into visiting a strip club near the interstate on the way home.

> *"I met someone there. We started talking and she asked what we did. We gave her a business card. A few months later she called me."*

From that moment on, Josh carried on a five-month affair with Alice until he eventually confessed to his wife and was removed from his church. A few months later in his downward spiral, he was arrested for driving under the influence.

It would be easy for anyone at this point to judge Josh and his decision. In fact, that's what his church did. In their hurt, anger and disappointment, they shut him out completely and never spoke to him again. His wife kicked him out of the house the day he confessed he was having an affair. Josh admits full culpability in what he did.

However, seven years before, Josh's life was filled with hope when he stood in the pulpit of a church with 30 people as their pastor in a rural Kansas town and began to preach the gospel. He didn't do it for the $600 a month they were paying him; he did it because he loved God and because he wanted to help people. How did Josh go from promising young minister with a young family to outcast?

Josh's story began as a young man when he felt the call to preach at the age twelve. Despite this call he went to college and pursued a financial career and started his own business. While he was in his late 20s, he returned to his calling and turned his financial business over to his partner, Matt. Josh and his wife Sue then began to seek the ministry in earnest. Sue was a licensed child psychologist and that enabled Josh to pursue the ministry at his own pace. They found a small church near Topeka where he was able to start a youth program. During that time, he began to preach at other local churches and learned that several were in need of a pastor. He was hired by a rural church about 40 miles outside of Topeka with 30 elderly members who had a desire to grow. Josh worked hard as pastor and also volunteered in other programs across the community while Sue found work in Topeka as a counselor. During the first few months, Sue gave birth to their second child.

The church grew quickly under Josh's leadership. Within a year, attendance doubled, they added a new service on a Sunday night. Josh said:

> "The church was growing, God was blessing."

They revamped their Vacation Bible School program so that attendance went from eight the previous year to 100 the next.

> "We had lots of growth and not just physically. People were learning, people were growing, and people were actively doing things. They were trying to find out what their gifts were and what their ministry needed to be."

Unfortunately, problems began to manifest during his third year of service. Josh was very busy in his work and did not see the dangerous signs of postpartum depression in his wife. It was a cycle that repeated itself everyday that became worse and worse for her:

> "There were a lot of things going on at work for her. I started watching her more closely. She started coming home and she would take the kids. I would have dinner waiting. We would eat, she would lie down with both of the kids crying until they all fell asleep. She'd wake up in the morning crying getting ready, she'd be off to work, then get back."

As Sue's depression worsened, Josh began to sink with her. The church was having issues as well. The church had almost quadrupled in size which would be perceived as good, but with change often comes conflict.

> "There were lots of people that wanted change, there were lots of people who didn't; so I started getting met with resistance."

Specifically, Bob, one of his deacons who had initially given him a great amount of support at the beginning, was making it very difficult for him while the church grew rapidly and transformed into a younger, more vibrant place.

> "He was going into the community, he was going to breakfast with the other men and talking about all the 'horrible things' that were taking place at the church, all the things the 'new pastor' was trying to do and how he had no respect for the older generation, no respect for tradition. It was really becoming almost a daily obstacle when I was getting not just people from my church but now people from the community that know me, calling me and saying, 'You need to be aware that this is what's going on.'"

Josh tried to handle it diplomatically by convening the other deacons to have them confront Bob. However, when Bob would enter the room, all of them would back down to avoid a confrontation. Josh felt disrespected and frustrated with the leadership of his church. The conflict was unresolved and the gossip continued unabated. The pressure and expectations of the church, the community, self-expectations and problems at home were leading to burnout – or worse:

> "I don't think I had a nervous breakdown, but did I shut down for a while? Yeah. I shut down totally or else I wouldn't have made the choice to cheat on my wife and have the affair. That's irrational. That's not me. That's not the type of decision I've spent my life making. After one bad decision you start making more. Then you start reacting instead of thinking and acting."

Sue and Josh's intimacy worsened. Josh rued the days of their early marriage, before the depression and the conflicts of ministry.

> "We had a very strong relationship early on. We would both come home and would take a walk through our neighborhood, do a few laps, talk about our days. We had a very passionate, romantic life."

They also began to have financial problems. To counter this, Josh called Matt and asked if he could partner up with him again. They agreed to restart their partnership and began travelling and working together again.

It was during this time that Josh realized that there was a serious problem in his marriage. Sue and Josh had been saving together for a trip to Paris for their ten-year anniversary. He was hoping that the trip would rekindle their relationship and bring them closer together. However, he shared that the trip showed him his worst fears were confirmed:

> "It was being in Paris and sitting with my wife near the Eiffel Tower. I realized we weren't even holding hands. I looked at her and she was vacant. She was just gone. There was nothing. We were in the Louvre, looking at the magnificent works of art and there was still nothing. And so we flew back and I threw myself into work and into church. She threw herself into her job and we kept working."

It wasn't long after that when Josh had his encounter with Alice at the strip club. Alice lived close to Josh and his heart turned toward her.

"We started a phone conversation and a couple of months later it became a physical relationship. One night my wife and I got into a conversation and we were talking and the truth came out."

Sue kicked him out of the house and Josh said, "as she should have." He moved in with a friend of his and he says his life became one horrible decision after another.

"I began drinking to cope. My choices became horrible. I stopped caring about anything. I stopped working. I stopped doing."

The church was very hurt by his actions. Josh said the only person who ever spoke to him was an older woman in the church, Sarah, who still speaks to him today. Other than that, he was fully rejected for what he had done. He said even two years later, they still wouldn't look at him when he returns to the area:

"That hurts. These are people who I was there for when their families were hurting and they were grieving and when they made mistakes. And they will turn their back on me because I made a mistake. How else are they going to react? I told my church from the very first Sunday, 'I don't want you to ever put me up on a pedestal because I am flesh and blood, I am a man, I am going to make mistakes. Whether it is a huge, gigantic, life-altering mistake, or if it's just something stupid and simple like misquoting a verse. I'm going to make mistakes. So if you think that I'm perfect, I'm going to fall. And the fall is not going to be good.'"

Josh says there were three or four pastors who tried to reach out to him after his fall. They came into his secular place of work and tried to talk to him about his sin. However, he wasn't willing to listen to him as he was caught up too deep into his downward spiral.

"I was wallowing in self-hatred and misery, self-loathing. They tried. They would come and sit in my office where I

was working, but I wasn't ready to be reached out to at that point."

His relationship with Alice continued off and on for a couple of years after he resigned the church. Alice would call and stay with Josh for a few weeks, then disappear for a while. After a time, she would reappear, then disappear again. It was during that time that he got his DUI during a tumultuous day in which Sue, his parents, and finally Alice, all contacted him with troubling circumstances. He was driven to the brink by Alice and realized he needed change in his life:

> *"I discovered she was an addiction for me. A part of me saw this as what I gave up my marriage for and I didn't want it to slip away. So I put a lot more work in trying to make things work out there, but it was never going to. I knew it early on though, so I left and came back home. It was very much like going through a rehab process because I had to dry out from her."*

After two years he moved back to his hometown where his parents still lived. He hoped to recover his relationship with them and find steady work. During this process, he received a call from his ex-wife. She invited him over to watch the kids during the day. That gesture grew into him making dinner for all of them in the evenings and eventually into all of them attending family functions together.

> *"We had a good relationship again. She called me if she had trouble. I went to her if I needed advice. We were back doing that again. And, my relationship with my parents was restored."*

There was another relationship in Josh's life that hadn't been restored. He hadn't come back to knowing God and His grace since his fall. He described the moment as an "ironic" one that occurred on Easter Sunday. He didn't attend service with his ex-wife, parents and children, although his parents served his family dinner after the service. He was expecting his parents to come pick him up, but Sue came instead. He got into the car and he said she grabbed his hand and had some kind, yet intense words to share with him:

> *"She told me she was going to tell me something and I could take it or leave it. And if it made me mad then it made me mad. But she told me that I had been given a gift of being able to take the Word of God and explain it and make it accessible and applicable to people and that I was never going to find success and happiness until I re-embraced that gift, forgave myself and moved on. I thought that was a very astounding statement for my ex-wife to make."*

Josh knows that he is a different man after his affair in many ways, including the way he cares for people.

> *"I had become a very calloused individual. I was very numb. I did things without thinking of the consequences."*

He said that it especially manifested itself after his DUI. On that day when he had received a bevy of bad news, he retreated to a lonely spot, drank a large quantity of liquor and had settled in for the night until he received a call to drive somewhere. Under the influence, he decided to leave and received his ticket. He says many people questioned his decision making at that stage of life after his fall.

> *"People say, 'You could have prayed.' I could have prayed but I didn't need to pray at that point. I needed someone that I could see, that I could sit down with and I could talk to and get some bearings on. I just didn't think I had anyone."*

After time has passed and grace has been shown to him, he knows he's a different man. He spent a long time in the wilderness and came out a changed and humbled man with a passion to restore lost relationships and with remorse on how he hurt others.

> *"My outlook on other people has changed. I'm not as judgmental maybe as I once was. I never considered myself proud or arrogant but had any of that been in me, it's definitely not now. When you lose everything, when your house gets foreclosed on, when your car gets repossessed,*

when you lose a majority of your clothing, when you lose a
majority or your friends, when you lose your family, you just
don't have a reason to have self-confidence much less to be
proud or arrogant."

At the time of our interview, three years after his fall, Josh felt God was dealing with him and felt He might be leading him back into some sort of ministry. He wasn't sure what was going to happen with him and Sue, but he knew God was restoring relationships in his life. He understood the toll his fall had taken on him and was working on a restoring his former life. Josh said:

"I'm not ready to step into the pulpit. God is still working in
me and there are some relationships I have to repair. I miss
the man I used to be."

Section Three

Understanding The Fallen Pastor

To restore the fallen pastor and the fallen culture, it is important to understand why the pastor falls and the circumstances around his fall. It is easy to look down upon the sinful pastor at his worst moment as he is cast out of his place of ministry. But Christ's compassion calls all of us to stand beside the fallen, not listening to the crowd in its judgment, but reaching out to the one who is in need of help the most. In doing so, the sin is not excused. It is transcended through grace and forgiveness. The fallen pastor is given someone to walk with in hope of restoration.

Each of these stories contains a common thread of experience. All of these men carry their own responsibility for their sin. Each was a pastor because he felt called by God and was bound by a set of expectations that transcended the expectations most people live by. But the question of "Why?" still remains. What makes some pastors break the line of morality and others stay the course?

Many of the men interviewed shared sentiments like, "In all my years I never could have considered it before." But suddenly it seemed like the choice was there. In a moment of weakness preceded by years of living in a troublesome culture, their hearts turned to sin and they fell. These men even admitted that there had been opportunities to fall before, but they had been strong or not interested in the temptation that was offered to them.

These pastors crossed denominational lines, some had large churches, some had small churches, some had a seminary education and others didn't. All of them have the appearance of a love and devotion for Jesus Christ before they fell. They were in love with the ministry and their church at one point and had baptized people into the faith. Their passion for Christ was great and their love for what they were doing was strong.

During their time as pastor, each of them began to experience weakness while serving. A trap was being set for them and they were seemingly unaware and unprepared for the problems that lay ahead. Despite years of training and preparation for the ministry, hours of careful study of the Scripture, they fell and were cast out.

There is a need to understand the fallen pastor and his sin, but there is an equal need to understand the culture from which he fell. Fallen pastors are being churned out of an equally fallen culture each month and unless both are understood, the problems will continue. A pastor who is using a culture to supplement his ego is going to find failure. Equally, that culture will find it difficult to minister effectively.

In interviewing fallen pastors, there seem to be four areas of weakness that these men had in common. In each case the men shared a concern for at least three out of four issues. The four concerns are: High expectations, isolation, judgmentalism and a poor relationship with their spouse. The church's response to the pastor's fall will also be examined.

Chapter 14

High Expectations

Pastors are faced with one of the most difficult jobs in the world. They are hired to lead a group of people each week with varying political backgrounds, vast age differences, different ideas on Scripture and life and somehow bring them together in unity. His job is to make each church member and leader happy, make the church prominent in the community and preach the divine truth. Meeting high expectations are part of his job, or he might find himself looking for a new church.

Too often, the pastor stretches the words of the Apostle Paul, "I have become all things to all people" and makes them into a charge for ministry. He faces high expectations from his church, from himself and from his denomination and spreads himself out thinly to attempt to meet the needs of anyone who has a want or complaint. He has to be part politician, part public speaker, part family man and all Christ. In the midst of these expectations, he runs the risk of being seen as the idol of ministry perfection. In doing so, the expectations only become greater.

Drive through any growing town and you will see billboards asking you to come to a contemporary church's three morning services with events for the family, "Come visit our website!" Keep driving and you'll see competing church signs that point you to different events catered to your family's needs along with family event centers, gyms, large auditoriums and outdoor playgrounds. On top of that, you might even see a billboard with a snapshot of the church's smiling pastor, his wife and two lovely children.

Without a doubt, the pastor is the face of the American church and he is expected to be the captain of the ship. In many cases, he leads the way with a Facebook page, Twitter account and personal website. He dresses in public like he dresses behind the pulpit. If he's a suit and tie man, then he'll be a suit and tie man at Wal-Mart. If he's a trendy t-shirt and jeans guy, that's how you'll see him at Starbucks. The pressure is on him all day, every day to be the pastor. As Dominic, the pastor who reached the breaking point, shared:

> "We live in a fishbowl. We live in a world where we have to be careful what we say, who we say it to, where we go, who we go with, how we're seen, how we're dressed – all of that to us is a pressure cooker."

Pastors are often viewed as heroes in their roles. Whether they are the men on the billboard or the powerful speaker behind the pulpit, they are often greatly admired by their congregation. Each week, they are the ones bringing forth the Word of the Lord amplified by a microphone for all to hear. He has answers to life's problems, baptizes the sinners, takes time for the children, has a beautiful family, and seems to have everything going for him.

For many pastors, the place behind the pulpit is powerful. Before their ministry began, they were not seen as strong or outspoken men. But after being called to preach and receiving a seminary education, they become empowered. Each week, they proclaim the words of God and receive praises and affirmation from the congregation. Without proper reflection dosed with humility, the pastor will find himself in a trap of pride and idolatry.

To many, he is bulletproof. He stands high upon a platform and has a great amount of biblical knowledge and is like a modern day prophet. Sometimes, he is idolized. For many, he becomes an idol, an example of what they should be and who they should become. He becomes their hero or role model. Some hang on his every word and brag about him, "You should have heard what our pastor said last Sunday!" For some women, he becomes a model of what their husbands should be, "Why can't you be more like our pastor? He has it all together!" In their book, Preventing

Ministry Failure, Michael Todd Wilson and Brad Hoffmann address this very issue:

> "Ministries and congregations in many ways treat their ministers like gods. The average parishioner would likely deny such 'worship,' but their actions sometimes demonstrate a misplaced sense of trust (not to mention pressure). Why else would they become so upset when we don't measure up to their unspoken expectations of perfection? Why else would so many leave – not just an organization but their faith altogether – when a minister is exposed for moral indiscretion? No longer are we seen as human beings with feet of clay who have a special calling to lead or preach the gospel. No, for some the minister has become a god, placed high on a pedestal. This is a great danger in ministry."[9]

Pastors know they are being idolized too. They know they are being looked up to. It is more than appreciation and more than a simple, "thank you." It happens when a pastor craves that extra attention or is in need of appreciation. They agree to the "idolization" of the pastor, sometimes knowingly or unknowingly. It happens to many pastors, whether they end up in adultery or not. It feeds their pride and makes them feel appreciated and validates their role as pastor, especially when conflict occurs.

It is a dangerous thing to be in this position. It is a trap of false affirmation from the congregation and false affirmation of self to feed one's own anxiety and self-need. Wilson and Hoffman commented on this cycle:

> "We put on an air of confidence, even though on the inside we're fearful of letting them down. We know we don't deserve their accolades, but even if it's not quite true, it does make us feel good about ourselves for a while."[10]

Pastors tend to have a need for approval from others, just like any other person. Many of them do not receive this affirmation at home. Some begin with a low self-worth and find gratification when they preach. The appreciation they feel from the culture of ministry feeds them but it does not satisfy their need completely. Vincent, the Methodist pastor, shared his addiction to appreciation before he fell:

> "It's like taking heroin. You need more and more and more.
> The insecurity comes back more strongly each time."

The insecurity that returns needs a stronger affirmation. In the ministry culture, a church may place the pastor on a pedestal. He feeds off the appreciation of the church and may not be doing so selfishly. It may seem harmless to him and it may not seem prideful, as he may perceive that he is just fulfilling a need to feel appreciated. But as the church praises him and places higher expectations on him and he increases his own workload and accepts their accolades without exception, he wanders into a trap of idolatry and almost undesired perfection. Joe, the pastor who fell after he discovered his wife's adultery, acknowledged his place as an idol:

> "I was the savior. They had me on a pedestal. Almost in the
> place of an idol. It was too high. Ministers like that. We like
> the praises of people."

This idol worship has created the opening for a fall. The church has helped create a pastor who is larger than life and the pastor has agreed to their false image of him. He has no need to humble himself or bow before God because his affirmations are constantly being fed. However, if conflict arises in the church or a catastrophe occurs in his own life, he may begin to seek out the need for extra affirmation. He will grow angry with his wife for not providing affirmation for him and become unstable at home. He may seek affirmation through a chosen vice, pornography or adultery. He may not have ever had an urge for those things before, but now there is a void of affirmation. Whatever he does pursue, the sin is upon his head in the end, but his sin did not occur in a vacuum. He is not a victim, but his pride was nurtured by those unaware that he was a man desperately in need of humility, biblical support and close friendship.

The expectations of the pastor are high from the beginning. Every pastor is aware of the words of Scripture before they enter the ministry. When they take the mantle of their position, they are warned continually of the words from 1 Timothy 3:2 "an overseer must be above reproach," along with a litany warning them against public and private sins of the heart. Ministry is a serious thing to engage in and all pastors are wary of their task. The unrealistic expectations that drive the pastor come primarily from their church and from themselves.

Expectations of the Church Membership

The needs and expectations of the congregation are many and weigh heavily upon the mind of the pastor daily. It can be an overwhelming experience to be a shepherd to a crowd of voices competing for attention with varying needs, concerns and complaints. Pastors often internalize the expectations that the church membership and leadership place upon him even when church is not in session. These expectations can either be handled with care and readiness, or with stress and disastrous results.

The pastor has many duties to fulfill on a weekly and daily basis. In any denomination, these duties are expected to be carried out and may vary depending upon church size and may increase or decrease based on the needs of the week. Tasks include daily prayer and devotion, visitation of those in nursing homes, visitation of the sick in the hospital, visitation of church members who are not able to leave their homes, visitation of the ill in their home, visitation of new members, visitation of prospective members, preparation of at least three messages a week, staff meetings, meetings with associational boards, regular committee meetings within the church, counseling, taking calls from members with concerns or prayer requests, conducting funerals and weddings, deacons meetings, preparing for business meetings and any other number of tasks that may arise.

George Barna took note of the litany of tasks pastors handle on a regular basis:

> *"Our studies show that church-goers expect their pastor to juggle an average of 16 major tasks. That's a recipe for failure. Trained in theology, [pastors] are expected to master leadership, politics, finance, management, psychology, and conflict resolution."*[11]

It would seem that dealing with people in committee to affect change is one of the pastor's primary roles. Even if the pastor is able to step away from these committees, he is still affected by conflict that may arise. His finger is constantly on the pulse of the church and he constantly fields questions about the happenings of his local congregation.

The Fuller Institute of Church Growth reported that 40% of pastors expressed a serious conflict with one church member at least once a month and 90% feel inadequately trained to cope with the demands of ministry.[12] Pastors can often get mired down in the demands of church "career management" and become frustrated with business rather than ministry. Pastor and author Mark Roberts noted how expectations can lead to a crisis:

> "For those of us who are maybe a little insecure with not a great sense of self, we try to live up to [high expectations], we overwork, we don't take the best care of our families and pretty soon we've got a problem. I think that contributes to one of the factors that can get people into the place of vulnerability, emotionally, spiritually and physically. Then their guard is down."[13]

For instance, one of the high expectations of some churches is visitation. It may seem strange to a non-pastor that visitation can bog a minister down, especially if the church is small or if the pastor has a staff. Most pastors prioritize preaching as their top activity, but realize the necessity of visitation of the sick and prospective members. The church may also have a spoken or unspoken high expectation for the pastor to visit older members on a regular basis. The process can be time consuming and can divide the pastor's duties. If the pastor does not visit on par with the church member's expectation, complaints can arise and more pressure can result. Dominic shared this insight:

> "The expectation of some senior members weighed heavily. They would say, 'You ought to go out and see Lida Mae.' I'd say, 'Why?' They'd say, 'You just need to go see Lida Mae.' I tried to train the congregation on what a good preacher was; either one who was preaching powerful messages

from the pulpit or visiting all the time. They couldn't have
both. People just have all these unspoken expectations."

Sadly, with the division of all of these tasks, something is suffering in the life of the American pastor. His attention is being shifted toward his preaching, visitation, pastoral duty, committee meetings and the ministry and away from his devotional time with God and his family. The Francis Schaeffer poll found that 72% of pastors only studied the Bible when preparing for a sermon and 77% of them felt they did not have a good marriage. The expectations placed upon the pastor can lead to stress, depression and burnout. The Francis Schaeffer Institute of Church Leadership reported that 90% of pastors expressed feeling frequently fatigued and worn out on a daily or weekly basis.[14] The stresses of the ministry are leading many pastors down a road of illness, isolation and far worse.

Jake Larson, ministry leader at XXXChurch.com and co-founder of Fireproof Ministries shared one of his pastoral experiences:

> *"I was at a traditional church when I was senior pastor and*
> *it was an absolute nightmare. And I had people around me*
> *all day. And part of the part of the problem was I couldn't*
> *get people away from me. My door was constantly open. Yet*
> *I was more alone in that journey, but I had a team around*
> *me, than anything I had done in my life because ultimately*
> *I'm getting shot for everything that happens. I'm constantly*
> *alone. I'm wondering, 'Was that the right decision?' The*
> *pressure you live under is detrimental."*[15]

Expectations of Self

Regardless of the expectations church members or leadership may place upon a minister, they pale in comparison to the expectations he places on himself. Aware of the high expectations placed before them, pastors often choose to work longer hours, demand more of themselves and live a more stressful lifestyle. George Barna discovered that pastors are often more demanding of themselves than parishioners:

"When asked to rate the church's ability to help people grow spiritually, pastors were significantly less likely (6%) than churchgoers (33%) to give the organization high marks, reflecting the fact that pastors are often their own toughest critics."[16]

Most of the pastors who were interviewed reflected this kind of internalized pressure. Their stress led them to the outward action of striving to please the church and membership increasingly and in turn, making them vulnerable to ministry failure.

Vincent said, "I was on a huge pedestal and I internalized a lot of expectations about being a perfect pastor and having a perfect organization."

Shannon had the outward pressure of being broadcast on the radio and being the facet of a large Sunday school program, but most of the pressure that was derived in his life was from within: "I demanded a lot of myself. I was a perfectionist. It wore me out."

Denny, who was constantly at odds with his denomination, said his drive came from a slightly different need: "I had a real need to be accepted. It's a strength and a weakness of mine. It's a sense of not being accepted."

Bill Leonard, Director of Ministerial Care of the Church of God, separates ministers who are at high risk for immorality into two different types. The first are ministers who are depressed and tired and "their brain is suffering from the lack of pleasure."[17] The second group is made up of successful pastors. To them, success is like a drug addiction. Leonard said these pastors are always demanding a little more of themselves, most often measured in terms of their weekly attendance figures. When these pastors have an increase in church attendance, they want more each time and the "pleasure center of the brain is always adjusting to success." This causes an increased need for pleasure each time in the heart and mind of the pastor, creating in them possible room for temptation.

Those same expectations of self-success can breed in the heart of the narcissistic personality and create a dangerous combination. Many contemporary pastors are following the trends set by megachurch pastors and those who are most visible in society. Denny said he was doing things in his pulpit before they were popular. He had removed the pulpit and was preaching on a barstool before it was popular, as it is in today's culture. Pastors are very self-conscious and aware of what other pastors are doing and it affects the way they feel about their own church and their own ministry. Megachurch pastor Kris knew this pressure well:

> "Pastors are just so insecure. It's the only job in the world where your shareholders have a chance to get to you every week and tell you their thoughts. It is a peeing contest. We're judged on success – how big our church is, how big the offering was, how many buildings we've built. The fact of the matter is there are very few pastors that are going to have large churches. So everyone else feels like a failure. I was just in a church last week that had 400 people and the pastor said, 'I'm a failure.' I said, 'Why?' He was comparing his church to the church across town that ran 5,000. We're so insecure. That's why we want to be liked, we're in the people business. 1,000 people could tell me I did a wonderful job on Sunday but the one who told me I did a horrible job is the one I'm focused on."

A common refrain among pastors is that in order to become a preacher of renowned, one must copy the more popular ministers of today, including dressing and following their homiletic style. Southern Seminary Professor Dr. York warns against this and its repercussions for a fall:

> "If you have a narcissistic personality where a guy is very image conscious and he's always looking at himself through the eyes of other people; he's always got to wear the right clothes, got professional pictures of himself done for his church brochure and his Facebook page, that guy fits into a specific personality type that often commits adultery."[18]

Some churches will function with the pastor as the CEO performing a large number of the tasks and finding it difficult to delegate any to the church leadership or membership. At times, the pastor is unwilling to delegate tasks, which puts him in the same situation of frustration and anxiety. Either way, the church finds itself not working together as a body of believers each with unique abilities and assigned tasks, but instead as a ship sailing with a lone captain attempting to man all stations at once. Steve Reed, pastor, author and mentor to many fallen pastors, recognized the issues involved and knows the situation ministers place themselves in:

> "To me, it's almost like a set up. I'm becoming more and more convinced that the office of pastor is unbiblical in the sense of the way we do it. We put the guy on the pedestal and make him feed us every Sunday and make him do all the heavy lifting on teaching and we just isolate him more and more. And the more successful he gets, the more isolated he gets and therefore, the less accountable."[19]

According to Rodney Cox, CEO of Ministry Insights, some of the high self-expectations the pastor places upon himself comes from a lack of training in the area of leadership most ministers should receive in seminary. Many pastors have the idea that when Paul told the Corinthian church that he became "all things to all people,"[20] the application is for them to handle every task in the church singlehandedly. Paul's words were meant to be instruction on how to win some to Christ by living within their culture yet being free in Christ to do so. However, this verse has become a platform for pastors to drive themselves into the ground, performing all the acts of the body of Christ instead of just his own. Cox said:

> "We're not teaching that senior pastor that they don't have to be all things to all people. We're really not teaching a leadership model in the seminary that says, 'You need to lead from your strengths, you need to empower others to do the same and you need to be willing to invite others into your weakness and you need to challenge others to do the same. That's interdependence. That's the truth that we can do nothing apart from Christ, the whole spirit of interdependence. But we don't have a spirit of interdependence in the church today, we have a spirit of dependence and it's killing the church. It's killing pastors."[21]

The pressure to be the "do it all pastor" may become unbearable and he may become angry and frustrated with the church or her leadership. He may lash out at the church in his sermons in a passive aggressive manner or during leadership meetings. In Dominic's case, he reached out by handing out books on burned out pastors to his leadership team, but his veiled message fell on deaf ears. Many pastors are afraid of confessing weakness to a congregation or seeking out help. There's a reason most pastors don't reach out. Bill Leonard explains why:

> *"There were times I wanted to conclude my message by saying, 'Today I'm the greatest one among you who needs help. So I'm going to come down to the altar and I'm going to let you pray me through.' But we're performers. And sister so-and-so just met you at the door and said, 'I'm going to do whatever it takes to get rid of you.' And then we go to the pulpit, carry that moment in our hearts and we say, 'Good morning! How are you?' And on the inside we feel like dead meat because we're human beings."[22]*

The statements pastors make after leaving the ministry reveals the overwhelming internal stress they are experiencing. When a fallen pastor is relieved of his ministry, he often expresses a sense of relief from the exhaustive stress of the ministry and the overwhelming expectations. The Francis Schaeffer Institute states that 57% of pastors would leave the ministry if they had a better place to go[23], including a secular line of work. Rodney Cox, in his experience of aiding burned out and hurting pastors had heard one pastor say, "I would have been willing to stand on the back of a garbage truck instead of having to walk through the doors of my church and have to go back to work."[24] Some of the interviewed pastors confirmed the relief they felt of being done with the pastorate. Dominic said on some level, it was a relief to be out of the ministry:

> *"I didn't have to worry about the phone ringing for a funeral or an illness or any deacon's meetings, attendance. I didn't have to worry about all these things that plague our souls in ministry."*

One of the recurring topics in the interviews among pastors and experts was that many ministers seem to be seeking after the ministry as a career instead of Christ as a person. If this is occurring, the internal pressure of the pastor may not only be misguided, but it will also create greater feelings of insufficiency, self-doubt and self-pressure. Ironically, pastors are typically unaware of the problem beforehand, but they are able to recognize it after their fall with the help their counselors. Troy Haas, leader of one of the most intensive pastoral restoration teams in the country identified the problem:

> "So many guys, their identities get wrapped up in ministry and they end up serving and just forget what it meant to be a Christian, a believer, a member of the body of Christ, a member of a spiritual community."[25]

After his fall, Kris seemed to have a new perspective on this issue. When he was pastoring, his drive was for church growth for his ends and means, not for God's. In reflection, he understood the danger of it:

> "I realize everything is not about me now. I still struggle with insecurity but I work through it. I'm learning who I am in Christ. It's not what I look like or how big my church is. My identity is not wrapped up in my church. That's been huge to me. There's nothing I can do to impress God. He's not impressed with how big my church is. He's not impressed with how many people I baptized this year. The Southern Baptist Convention was impressed every year. But God wasn't."

High expectations are part of the culture that can lead the pastor into a dangerous place if he is not careful. High expectations from church membership and from himself can compound over time to create an overwhelming situation. Without proper perspective, the pastor can fall into behaviors such as narcissism, inflated ego and withdrawal.

To serve the church of our Lord Jesus Christ should not be viewed as a laborious thing. It is a rewarding thing to pursue as a pastor and minister even through difficulty and trial and it is worth the trouble. Many pastors become overwhelmed when they perceive they are the only ones participating in the growth of the church and feel the expectations of others. This may not be the complete truth as the church may be functioning together as a body, but this may be the pastor's own self-perception. However, this does become an issue when the pastor becomes isolated from his spouse and with no trusted friends to confide in.

Chapter 15

Isolation

The culture that surrounds the pastor often forces him into a place of isolation. High and unrealistic expectations, idolatry and stress often leave him stranded in a place where he is alone with no one to relate to. Often, he does not realize he is isolated until it is too late. The ministry friends he once had are gone, the strong relationship he once shared with his wife has disappeared and he struggles to find anyone to share his problems and concerns with. The pastor has fallen into the trap of isolation and is one step closer to a fall.

Despite the social networking society in which we live, pastors are not as connected as they seem. They may send out lots of Twitter messages per day, but probably have fewer real friends than their Facebook page reflects. The Fuller Institute of Church Growth's research indicated that 70% of pastors do not have someone they consider a close friend.[26] George Barna's research states "a majority of pastors (61%) admit that they 'have few close friends.'"[27] He also stated in research that, "pastors are nine times more likely to seek reactions to their sermon than they are to assess the congregation's reactions to visitors."[28] This might indicate that pastors are seeking some sort of acceptance on a superficial level when what they really need is a deep, meaningful, nurturing friendship where they can cultivate reciprocation of their communication. Pastors are needy people just like their congregants and in need of real relationships.

Many pastors find difficulty forming friendships within their community or their churches. Some find that within the church culture there is a lack of trust between pastor and congregant. Jake Larson made this observation about pastors sharing intimate issues within the congregation:

> "[One of the problems] in church ministry is that it's not safe, there's no place to go share burdens, there's no place to go to talk about the fact that you and your wife are intimate only once every three months. It's not working for you, now who to tell? It's your secret. Because you can't talk to anybody, and the church, as much as they say it's about grace and love, church people will turn on you faster than worldly people. Pastors learn that on in their ministry years and put up safety nets and those safety nets actually end up hurting them instead of helping them."[29]

If this attitude is a correct reflection of how most pastors feel, and it was consistently how most of the fallen pastors felt during our interviews, then what recourse do they have? Some pastors do go outside their church to make friends with fellow ministers or leaders, but even then, it is difficult. The difficulty, however, may not lie in the people the pastor is attempting to connect with, but with the pastor himself. Pastor and author Mark Roberts stated that it is difficult for pastors to have close friendships within the church:

> "Isolation is a factor. Sometimes we do that for ourselves or choose it for ourselves but partly there's a recognition of the relational limitations when they are in church. There are certain things that would not be appropriate to share within the context of the church, but where do you turn? Does a pastor have a place to go when he's really struggling with certain types of temptations or when he's doubting his faith? I think pastors have a great need to have a context where they can be open and fallible with their temptations, weaknesses and failures. Ideally, that would be a small group of other pastors, it could be in some kind of mentoring relationship with a mature pastor. But it's going to take some effort to make it happen. Most folks are in independent churches, but not only that, there's going to be

*some kind of effort where they realize it's important and say,
'This is something that I really need to do.'"*[30]

Who can the pastor trust? Denny's leadership group was made up of some
of his closest friends. They were men he trusted most in his life. When they
confronted him with his sin, he told them everything he had done and
asked them not to tell his wife until he had a chance to. Within 24 hours, one
of his closest friends had betrayed him. Joe's close friend and mentor was
the harshest critic of his adultery and disclosed his sin to the congregation
the night he found out. Joe said that after years of attempting to reconcile,
"it still doesn't change his mind because I embarrassed him, I lost reception
with him." It is a very difficult thing for a pastor to attempt to make close
friends with a church member or leader in the church. Dominic, a pastor
called later in life, had some wise insight into the matter:

> *"They recommend accountability groups and that's all well
> and good but it's just not realistic. A pastor in any group is
> still a pastor. If he can get a group of friends who are not
> part of his congregation it can be a different story. Most
> pastors don't have a lot of non-congregational friendships
> and some of the ones they do have go back to seminary so
> they're fellow pastors. Not a lot of pastors hang out with
> friends or fellow pastors especially if they're in small towns.
> Their ability to network and meet people is somewhat
> limited."*

Megachurch pastor Kris surrounded himself with staff members who were
his own friends who he knew would never keep him accountable. He also
knew that his relationships with fellow pastors were nothing more than
superficial:

> *"I had a select group of 'yes men' around me. And a select
> group of pastors who all were my friends, but they really
> weren't my friends, they were acquaintances. They weren't
> there when my world fell apart. They disappeared all of a
> sudden. Now, I have some of the healthiest friendships I've
> ever had in my life. I never thought I'd have friends like I do*

now. They keep me accountable, they get in my face and they're there for me. That's new to me to have true friends."

Some pastors avoid accountability simply because they do not want to have to answer to anyone. There can be an air of pride among some pastors who feel they are in command of the church and are so far above reproach that they need not answer to anyone. These men may be labeled by some as narcissistic in nature and exhibit traits of dominance and overwhelming need of power. Mark Roberts addressed the issue:

"In what ways are pastors truly accountable for the way they live their lives, their personal lives, their moral lives, even their theological lives? Some churches tend to have more structures of accountability, often more independent churches don't and sometimes there's accountability within an independent church to the board of deacons or elders. But a lot of times it seems the pastor is kind of the king and that can be a formula for disaster, but not in every case. There are of course, wise pastors who have authority and don't abuse it, but I think in general we need to be accountable to one another and submitted to one another after the Lord and that can help us be the kind of leaders and pastors and husbands we want to be."[31]

What is the main ingredient that leads pastors to become isolated in the first place? Pastors will probably always find excuses to avoid authentic relationships. It takes time and trust; two commodities many pastors are lacking. Ministers are surrounded by people in their church, community and have pastor friends who are probably willing to build relationships with them. Rodney Cox has spent years researching the issue. One of his main messages is that pastors should be willing to admit their weaknesses and rely on others to help them. However, our communities of faith are often filled with attitudes of judgment toward one another:

"What creates isolation? Judgment. I would say that we've lost sight in the church of living out the gospel of repentance and reconciliation. Because as soon as we repent, we're judged."[32]

Troy Haas, after meeting with many fallen pastors, noted that one of the most identifying characteristics of a fallen pastor is his isolation from authentic relationships. Pastors have friendships and accountability relationships, but often lie their ways through them, Troy states:

> *"What causes a guy to walk in freedom and walk in purity no matter what his background or unmet state of life is authentic spiritual community. Yet most pastors don't have that. Either by choice, by necessity or just by circumstances."*[33]

The pastor performs task after task that is oriented to giving to others, which he is called to do. This continual process of giving often causes the pastor to feel empty, especially when he is denying himself time in Bible study or prayer. Bill Leonard stated that the primary reason pastors fall is that they "lose their intimacy first with God." Between burning himself out and losing closeness with God, the pastor begins to yearn for increased intimacy. Sometimes, pastors begin to realize that there are problems in their life but also realize they don't have real friends to reach out to. They may seek out friends, but if they don't have accountability with those friends, they will be little help. Troy Haas stated:

> *"Even if you seek spiritual community outside the church, you aren't talking about 'real stuff.' So when you find yourself feeling lonely, discouraged, inadequate and in need for comfort, there's no one that knows that in your life. There's no one that's able to speak truth into that setting. So you begin to look at your secretary or a neighbor woman or whomever. When there is no authentic spiritual community in your life which God created, you're going to go down those paths."*[34]

Isolation, Conflict and Grief

Another factor that leads to isolation is unhealed pain and wounds from past hurt and grief. When the pastor is isolated, he may tend to view past hurt in two ways. One, he may be isolated and alone as Paul was in his story. He felt that he was left alone to grieve and there was no one to listen to his hurt. There are also those ministers who feel that because of their high status in the church culture, they can deal with the grief on their own. They become their own counselor and push the grief aside, denying any outside help. Troy Haas related the following:

> "We're all wounded, but if we don't face and deal with those wounds, we're just asking for trouble. So many guys just assume that all this stuff will go away and it won't matter."[35]

Pastors know unresolved pain from church experience. The Francis Schaeffer Group survey reported that 78% of pastors have been asked to resign their position at some point. Many pastors perform their parent's funerals and do not take the necessary time to grieve their deaths. Bill Leonard states that this is not the way to do things:

> "When we try to counsel ourselves, we can cancel ourselves out. We try to pastor ourselves, when we need the Great Shepherd, to read His Word every day and speak to Him and to someone who understands our situation who is confidential."[36]

It is possible that pastors feel a need to be the spiritual giants within their own church and will "write their own prescription" for their pain. Instead of seeking help, they crawl within their own hole of isolation. It is also possible that some within the church may feel that the pastor is capable of handling his own issues, as was the case with Paul, or they feel they are inadequate to help him in his grief. So, when tragedy and grief strike and pastors aren't finding comfort in their church, their God or their spouse, they may wrongfully look elsewhere. Pastors who go untreated through counseling or do not feel they need help may be at the highest risk. Dr. Hershael York shared a biblical parallel:

> "We find in Genesis 24 when Abraham's servant brings Rebekah back to Issac and he took her into Sarah's tent and he was comforted after the death of his mother. I think sex is a very comforting thing. Some guys commit adultery because there is a grief going on in their life."[37]

Not only does tragedy have an effect upon pastors, but conflict causes isolation as well. Several of the pastors interviewed had major conflicts at the same time of their fall or within a reasonable time period. These conflicts can cause unresolved hurt and may place the minister in the middle of a difficult situation where he may feel the need to play peacemaker between two rival groups within the church. Denny's constant conflict with his denomination was one of the contributing factors to his fall. The state board called him to answer for his church's actions several times which strained his own need for acceptance: "All that added a lot of stress that brought my weakness to the forefront."

Dominic's conflict with his church over finances and a building program with the leadership was one of the factors that led to his fall. He found himself constantly fighting with a small, powerful group of leaders who would not relinquish control over simple issues in the church. The arguing was contrary to Dominic's nature since he was a builder and a nurturer: "I had to become a real tough guy." Many good things were occurring in the church, but the leadership kept pressing him about issues they thought were important. He finally broke down in the midst of church conflict and a failing marriage:

> "There came a point where no matter how much Scripture I claimed I was just losing it. My marriage had gotten worse. I got to a point where I was just emotionally beaten up. I finally got to a point where I meant it when I said it, 'I just can't do this anymore.' I lost my drive."

Church conflicts may be more harmful to pastor/leadership relationships than a moral fall. Troy Haas reported that some broken pastors and their former churches were able to reconcile years later, although the percentage was relatively low. However, he did note that among the men he had known who had been counseled after a church split, none of them had ever been able to reconcile in any way with their former church because of the levels of anger that had been produced. The amount of unhealed anger and hurt that ministers carry around has a tremendous effect upon whether they follow the road to moral failure.

Isolation creates a terrible weakness in the life of the pastor. When he attempts to take on problems by himself, deal with his own hurt and grief without any outside help and does not forge any authentic friendships, he places himself in a dangerous place. The pastor's life is not able to withstand such tremendous pressure by himself over a long period of time.

When isolation does occur and pastors realize they have no solid friendships inside or outside the church, it is easier for them to make strong, inappropriate relationships with members of the opposite sex.

Chapter 16

Poor Relationship With Spouse

Unfortunately, the image a pastor may portray from the pulpit as a man who "has it all together" may be a deceiving one. This should not be surprising as many parishioners often hide their problems behind a smile on Sunday morning. Pastors and their wives deal with the same marriage and communication issues that their church members do, but the church may not always see it that way.

For almost all of the men interviewed, the culture of the church played a significant role in the downfall of their marriage, specifically in the communication and intimacy with their spouse. As the demands they perceived from the ministry grew, they placed more time and effort into their work, leaving less time for their spouse. Communication about church issues and problems became difficult and over time, sexual activity declined or ceased completely. None of the fallen pastors placed the entire blame on their spouse. Instead, most placed the burden of it upon themselves. One even blamed all of the communication and intimacy issues on himself.

Many churches have a tendency to have high expectations of their pastors, but they also tend to have high expectations of their families as well. This can cause a strain upon not just the pastor, but his wife and their marriage if they allow it to. The same difficulty that a pastor faces in making authentic friendships can also be true for the spouse. Dominic had an excellent observation about the struggles of ministry and the role of the pastor's wife:

"Pastoring is tough at best. Even if you have the great support at home and even if you have the quintessential pastor's wife it's still hard; if you don't have it, it's almost impossible."

Several patterns arose within the interviews regarding communication and intimacy issues. First, many pastors struggle with what they perceive to be a lack of appreciation from their spouse in contrast to the praise they receive from their church. Imagine the pastor on Sunday, leaving his pulpit and receiving praise from his parishioners, being hugged by the children of the congregation, told by his staff what a remarkable job he has done, thanked by members for his wise counsel and smiled at by each passing face. The pastor then retires to his home where his wife says, "You didn't pick your underwear off the floor again yesterday. And by the way, the trash needs to be taken out." He might reply, "What did you think of my sermon?" His wife shrugs her shoulders after having heard every word of his 500 previous sermons since he was ordained and says, "Not bad." Jake Larson said he had seen this type of relationship before:

"I'm [a great leader at church], but when I'm home I don't get that same treatment. If you can get good stuff from people at work from email and then you come home and you have to actually put the money where your mouth is. A lot of guys go, 'I don't need that.'"[38]

The pastor can also become overwhelmed with the high expectations of the church, worrying about his performance. He may have had to argue with two or three church leaders and been consumed with whether or not the church took in enough offering for the day. He may feel ragged and tired when he hits the door and wants to connect with his spouse on a simple level. However, neither the pastor nor his wife has the energy. Larson also recognized this opposite case as a common occurrence:

"In church ministry, you can never be good enough. You can strive to succeed but it's never quite enough. There's always someone who says, 'That wasn't good enough.' As men, there's a strive for success and ego and pride where we want to do great things. You live with this constant idea of

'I'm not going to be good enough' or 'I wonder if that was good enough.' And I think it plays into our egos, it plays into our self-esteem, then we go home and we need quick self-esteem and we don't want to put the work in because at work all we're doing is constantly fighting to gain people towards our mission or for our own personal approval and I think it just wears you down. I can't keep up with this constant stress and battle of trying to be good enough. Because everything I do I fall short. I come home, all I want is easy. And relationships aren't easy. So it's much easier to just look at porn or find some other way to release that pressure."[39]

If the pastor is in the wrong state of mind or his relationship with his wife is strained, he may take her comments to be cold and rigid, especially when he compares them to the high regard in which he is held at his church.

If not viewed correctly, the relationship with his wife may lead to two different types of problems. First, over time he may see his wife as uncaring or apathetic toward him or his ministry. His relationship with her is completely different than that of anyone in the church. She sees his many faults, washes his smelly clothes, smells his morning breath, sees him when he is angry and is privy to his darkest secrets. At home, he's not the pastor. He comes down off his pedestal and becomes a normal person who doesn't always smell good and snores when he sleeps. If he does not continually keep the uniqueness of his relationship with his wife in mind, he may tend to become hurt when her feedback is lacking.

Also, if there is an intimacy issue that exists for other reasons in the marriage, her comments and perceived lack of support may consciously or subconsciously feed his need for acceptance elsewhere. Many of the pastors interviewed showed signs of a need for constant acceptance and appreciation. When a pastor and his wife begin to lose intimacy, he may be more open to the praise of a female staff member or parishioner than he would have been before. Larson recalled one pastor who found his needs of acceptance in his church much to the detriment of his marriage:

"I know someone who fell and was a senior pastor who had all his emotional needs met through the church. And he neglected to emotionally feed his wife when he was at home; how home became a place where he had to put the kids to bed or keep the lawn up or make sure the house was this way or that way and all of a sudden there was no more emotional connection at home. For some reason his wife ceased being his wife."[40]

The pastor can also create a lot of strife within his family dynamic when he places the priority of ministry duties over those of his family.

Gary, former New Orleans megachurch pastor, mentioned that he worked long hours at his church because he wanted to be thought of as successful and it took time away from his relationship with his wife.

"I didn't feel desired by my wife and she didn't feel desired by me. I never took a day off from church I was going to outdo the last guy who was there. I would work from early in the morning to late at night. I wasn't there for her and the kids."

Dominic said, "Over a long period of time, my career in ministry became my drive to the exclusion to my relationship at home."

Lance, music minister in Hawaii, was in a long-term marriage that lacked intimacy but found his greatest pleasure in his work:

"I just poured myself into ministry."

Another problem is that some pastors perceive they are more spiritually mature than their wives. This may be true but a lack of spiritual intimacy, whether real or perceived, can harm the relationship between pastor and spouse. The pastor may be providing spiritual leadership at the church, but he may fail to provide it at home and become frustrated with his spouse when she does not follow or grow with the rest of the congregation.

Shannon, the long time Sunday school radio teacher said:

"She seemed to ride on the coattails of my spirituality."

Paul, associate pastor and mentor, said:

"We did a great job of raising kids, we dealt with money tremendously, sex was fine; but the connection spiritually, emotionally, intellectually – my wife has always been intimidated by my spirituality."

Several of the pastors interviewed knew their marriages were in poor condition. They felt that they were in such poor shape that they would never improve. They knew after their fall that they should have done something to make their marriage better, but at the time they were willing to live in a status quo marriage and focus on their ministry. For them, it seemed to be a Catch-22 situation where they were miserable in their marriage and wanted to leave, but they knew they couldn't because if they did they would be disqualified from the ministry which they loved.

Dominic said:

"I knew if our relationship ever led to divorce, I could kiss the ministry goodbye."

Dathan said:

"I wasn't looking because looking wasn't an option. You don't get a divorce. A divorce would end my ministry. The rule is, 'You don't divorce. You don't commit adultery.' You're stuck."

Some pastors are willing to stay in a marriage where they are miserable in order to pursue ministry. At the same time, many pastors aren't willing to fix their marriage or seem blind to the damage the ministry is doing to their relationship with their spouse. On the outside, the couple seems content to attend church and keep appearances up for their parishioners while there is a less than perfect situation within their home.

Intimacy issues at home often lead to the man seeking out alternative sexual options. A survey from the Leadership Journal showed that 33% of pastors admitted to visiting a pornographic website in the past year.[41] Jake Larson has had the opportunity to speak with pastors across the country and talk to them about their struggles:

"I forget off the top of my head what the statistics are [concerning pastors and pornography use], but when we go out to dinner with a pastor after they've had us in, I don't think there's been a single pastor who hasn't told us he hasn't struggled with pornography or is not constantly fighting that battle. Nobody has ever said to me, 'That's never been a real issue for me but I wanted to bring you guys in to talk about it.' Literally every pastor I've talked to when they're honest for a moment, away from their church, sitting down and eating lunch will say, 'Yeah, I think this is great, there's not a person I don't know who isn't struggling with this and we need this.'"[42]

Dr. Kailla Edger performed a study of evangelical men who identified themselves as sexual addicts. Interestingly, she did not desire to focus her attention on church leaders, but solely on those in the regular membership of churches. However, after interviewing her subjects, she found "that every one of them still served in leadership capacities at some point in their churches, and most of the men did not seek leadership roles on their own."[43] She also discovered that for the majority, these men sought out sexual behaviors such as pornography, visiting strip clubs and visiting online sex chat rooms "as a way to feel affirmed."[44]

Leaders in the church and pastors who feel a strong need to be affirmed and perceive that they are not being affirmed at home will often seek out such behavior as a momentary thrill. In fact, several of the pastors I interviewed admitted to pornography addictions before their fall from ministry. There is a sense in which pastors who lack affirmation at home begin to search for that affirmation elsewhere. Jake Larson confirmed that the constant pressure of the ministry expectations, isolation and poor relationship with the spouse could lead a minister to a breakdown and wrongfully search for affirmation elsewhere:

"For most pastors, in today's age there's a striving for success that creates such a burden unlike anyone else feels or experiences, because in the church there's spiritual components that seem to be in play, and I think the striving

for success makes us sell out on boundaries that we said we'd never sell out on. Like a senior pastor before he starts a new job and says, 'I'm not going to be working 70 plus hours a week, I'm not going to deny my kids experiences because of the church, the church is not going to be my whole life,' and I think the church just asks for everything, it just sucks the life right out of you by removing all the boundaries that you said you weren't going to cross. It brings you to a place of exhaustion where you've deflated some of your most personal relationships, you're lacking an intimacy connection and you suddenly get the opportunity to find it somewhere else. Whether it's pornography or a relationship with a person, or strip clubs, or online conversations with women or text messaging, or whatever you want to call the infidelity. You're exhausted and you don't want to put that work into a real person so you find the easy way out." [45]

The Original Mistress

After studying each case, a surprising pattern emerged. Many pastors enter into a harmful culture where they are esteemed for their talent and eventually idolized. The pastor is given high expectations and over exerts himself to meet those expectations. In doing so, he strives to meet the needs of the church over all else in his life to please her. The church becomes his first mistress.

Over time, as he pushes himself to find acceptance and appreciation from the church, he finds that his spouse does not give him the same amount of accolades for him at home. Their communication breaks down as he may view her as moving in a different spiritual direction. He spends more time fulfilling the needs of his ministry than his family, or that may be the perception. This is the trap that many ministers fall into as they chase after their first mistress, the church. As the church eventually runs out of praise for him, he may become burned out, angry or fall into sexual temptation.

Two things begin to happen for the pastor who finds fulfillment from his ministry rather than at home. First, as his relationship with his wife suffers, he finds reasons to spend more time at work to fill in the gaps of appreciation and adoration that are lacking in his marriage. Secondly, as he finds more fulfillment in his work in the ministry, he becomes increasingly more critical of his relationship with his spouse and his marriage deteriorates.

The minister is often blind to this process while it is unfolding. The work and time he places into the ministry at the cost of his family is rationalized as being the "work of God" and he sees any consequence of it as a sacrifice that has to be made. As time passes and he becomes burned out, he eventually realizes that his relationship with his spouse has broken down and he cannot understand when or how it occurred. Consequently, he blames his spouse, her lack of spirituality or he may blame the ministry and may begin to seek affirmation elsewhere.

Another problem that may occur is when conflict or criticism arises within the church culture. When that happens, the pastor may feel betrayed by his ministry mistress. He reflects upon the countless hours he has toiled for her, prayed over her, visited her members and balks at the idea that criticism over his role as pastor could even be a thought in the minds of the people. The more prideful he is or the more severe the conflict or criticism, the more bitter he may become with his rumination. If he feels rejected, he may look for affirmation from another source.

Most pastors will not admit it, but they are fragile people, just like everyone else. They take their work seriously and are dedicated to their job. The trap is set when a minister begins to seek affirmation and comfort from their ministry career instead of viewing Christ as the source of their strength. If that line is crossed, they will find themselves with the ministry as mistress.

Contrary to popular thought, the ministry can actually be dangerous for a ministry couple. If the pastor begins to succumb to the pressures of the ministry, spend more time on his job than his family and chase after the wiles of the mistress of the church culture, he will find that his relationship with his wife will deteriorate quickly.

Chapter 17

Judgmentalism & Response To Ministry Failure

Reflecting on the story of the adulterous woman in John 8, most of the ministers before their fall would have found themselves alongside the Pharisees in the crowd holding stones in their hand. When their sin was discovered, they found themselves in the place of the woman, with only the compassionate Christ as friend. Their fall radically changed their outlook on how they treat people today and has moved them from a judgmental mindset to a redeeming and compassionate one.

Many of the ministers interviewed recognized that during their ministry, they had been overly judgmental toward people and harsh in their criticism toward church members. Some said that they had begun their ministry with a more compassionate outlook, but as conflicts arose in the church, they became more jaded with people.

Gary reflected upon a man whom he confronted while pastoring at his new church. The man had committed a serious crime and had been caught in the act. Gary talked with the man privately, showed compassion and walked with him through his sin. Gary said:

> *"If that had been before my fall, I would have unleashed on him."*

Lance loved the music ministry, but was forced into the role of pastor unexpectedly. He remained pastor for three years and after stress and problems, he found himself becoming increasingly judgmental:

"I was burned out but I didn't even know it. I really hated people all the time. That's a good sign you need to get checked out as a pastor."

During the time of their pastorate, they did not recognize judgmentalism as a problem in their life. Many of them grew up with strict interpretation of Scripture or legalistic backgrounds. The responses from the men interviewed reflects this:

Kris said:

"I'm a lot more compassionate. If you had given me a spiritual gift inventory before, mercy would have been dead last. I took one recently and it's number two now. I used to say I had a build a bridge philosophy – build a bridge and get over it. It's amazing now how my heart breaks."

Gary said:

"My fall has affected how I treat people. I know what shame is. I know its not fun. I still comfort but I try to love and restore."

Josh said:

"I find myself trying to be more understanding when people have problems."

A judgmental attitude is not the same as having a strong sense of discernment. Pastors should be able to recognize sin. Neither did these pastors use Scripture to justify their sin after their fall during their restoration process. The judgmental attitude they displayed was one that lacked compassion for those who sinned in their church before they fell. They used Scripture in a harsh manner toward some in their congregation who were caught in sin. Many described their life after their fall as being "more compassionate" and more "like Christ." Before their fall, they would have not shown compassion or patience toward sinners, but after their fall, they are patient and gracious toward sinners while helping them deal with their sin.

It is a question whether the pastor enters the ministry with a judgmental attitude or if it develops as a result of the ministry culture. Each pastor is different and both statements could be true. Each Christian is capable of displaying a judgmental attitude instead of one of compassion, hence Christ's command to "judge not" in the Sermon on the Mount. Whatever the case may be, it appears that some pastors may become more judgmental of people within their church as the years pass, conflicts arise, troubles build and pressures become greater.

When a pastor has an overly judgmental attitude, he shows signs of pride and moves toward arrogance. When he is in the pulpit, he may even feel invincible with his pronouncements. He often feels a need to control everything that happens within the church. He plays a strong hand with an overly strong black and white interpretation of Scripture or a "my way or the highway" view and often opposes those who disagree with him. Sometimes, the pastor may seem strong handed because of the perception of lack of work by the church.

When a pastor's complete involvement is coupled with a narcissistic personality, he may have increased expectations of appreciation and respect from those around him. When he does not receive them, he may perceive that he is being unappreciated by his church and those in his home. His harsh judgment may increase and his pride will increase with it, using the Bible as justification. His pride, as the Bible tells us, will come before a fall. When pastors perceive they are lacking appreciation when others do not agree with their pronouncements and hard line attitude, they may begin to seek comfort, affirmation or agreement elsewhere. All of this reflects a problem of the heart that leads ultimately to the pastor possibly falling into worse sin.

In Dathan's case, he realized that he had a very judgmental and legalistic attitude while pastoring. He performed duties while pastoring not out of love or compassion, but out of a sense of duty or command. There was no room for gray areas in his life, love or understanding. Those actions even spilled over into his marriage:

> "If you're being faithful to your wife because you're expected
> to as a rule, a red flag just got sent up. But if you're in love

*with your wife in a loving relationship and in love with the
Lord and not doing those things because you have to and
they're the rules, you have a much better chance of not
falling. Before, it was either black or white, there were no
gray areas for me."*

Both isolation and judgmentalism can cause tension within the pastor's life
and lead him further into the trap of moral failure. Seen together, a pastor
may tend to become angry and more judgmental when he feels alone and
rejected by people close to him. His judgmentalism will also push people
further away from him.

The Response to Ministry Failure

The final phase of the problem is the response to ministry failure. The pastor
has fallen into the trap due to his own will as well as the circumstances of
the culture around him. The response to his fall is a strong determinant as
to how and if the pastor is able to be restored to a basic level of Christian
fellowship. Christ's response in John 8 was compassion in the face of much
judgment. Too often, the response to the fallen pastor is one of anger and
estrangement, pushing him to the wilderness to be an outcast.

The church leadership provides the main response to the fallen pastor.
Everyone will be looking at how leadership handles the situation. When
the pastor falls, the church leadership is faced with an awful reality. They
are confronted with a human being who has committed a sin. It is a sin
committed by a person they loved and trusted. But the sin has been
committed by a person whom Christ loves and needs compassion. Church
leadership often turns away from a response toward the sinner and toward
a personnel decision.

What has been most notable throughout this research is how unprepared
church leadership is for the moral fall of a pastor. In the cases researched,
church leadership responded angrily and swiftly in all but one of the cases
and demanded a resignation and offered no counseling to the pastor or
couple. Many were immediately forced to leave town or clean out their
offices. In the case of Gary who pastored a church of over a thousand
people, he said:

"The church really didn't know how to handle it. They were clueless."

Lance, who also worked in a mega-church said:

"We were thrown away like garbage."

In his situation, the church was in the midst of a building project and felt as if Lance's leaving might affect the outcome. Looking from the outside, it seemed as if the church was protecting their image by removing the stain of Lance's sin by removing his presence. Lance said he felt like 99% of the membership still loved and embraced him, it was just the leadership that turned their back on him.

Church leadership handled the situation harshly for Joe. In Joe's case, he was exposed by his mentor who:

"swooped in, armed with a videotape. He forced me to resign and humiliated me in front of my church."

For Denny, after a supposed confidential meeting with church leadership, they called his wife and told her the sordid details of his affair. He said:

"I don't think the church is equipped to know how to deal with a pastor when he falls."

It is an understandable human response by the leadership when anger arises. When we are hurt or disappointed by those we placed faith or trust in, hurt quickly turns to anger. Nevertheless, that does not mean he the fallen pastor should be beyond some sort of restoration at the moment of his fall. Looking back to Christ in John 8, he stood between the angry mob and the adulterous woman. The mob demanded justice; Christ showed that true justice was found in compassionate restoration. Even if leadership cannot find instant forgiveness, hopefully they can look toward a model of restoration.

Churches do seem ill equipped to handle the mountain of emotions that befall them at the moment when they discover the pastor's sin. Despite overwhelming hurt and anger, grace needs to overwhelm all of us when a brother or sister falls into sin, as we all know we could easily find ourselves thrown accused at the feet of Christ one day.

The cycle of hurt seems to be a common and natural knee-jerk reaction when the pastor's sin is discovered. The sin is brought to the church leadership's attention and a meeting is often held to discuss the issue. If the pastor is brought in and his moral failure is discussed and he is asked for details, he rarely repents as he is on the defense and still mired in his sin. The pastor is forced to resign and often asked to leave the premises immediately. The church then meets as a whole to discuss the situation and they are told of his sin. All of these events take place in a relatively short time period and with great hurt and anger within the hearts of the leadership. The church members are not given much guidance or help on how to sort out these issues.

David Trotter shared his experiences in a book about his fall from ministry, "Lost and Found."[46] In an interview, I shared with him that an extremely small minority of fallen pastors are ever able to speak to their former congregants as a whole and find restoration. He then shared his ideas and frustrations concerning his fall:

> "Whoever the body of that congregation is, whether it's denominational oversight, there needs to be some predetermined path of response. Because a lot of churches when they find out, they start scrambling and it becomes a natural response of people to take over and want to shoot them. To have some sort of plan in place. And how does that involve grace, how does that involve all parties involved – and there's no hard and fast rules because they're so complex. But even when I reconciled with my wife I've never been able to reconcile with my church at any level. The problem with that is it throws the congregation under the bus because they don't have the opportunity to hear words that will free them up to move them up toward forgiveness. Because I wasn't allowed to give them the opportunity to give them that message, and people don't think I'm sorry, because I wasn't allowed to, it then creates those separations of relationships forever, a lot of pain and

> *a lot of awkwardness. Some sort of response is helpful and*
> *healthy."*[47]

What often occurs is within a week or two of the dismissal, a member of the deacon body or leadership team may question how the dismissal was handled or whether they should reach out to the pastor and give him some help. By that time, the pastor is gone and often bitter and angry and the church is full of hurt and anger as well. The church leadership makes the agreement that their decision was correct and often justifies it with a sentiment such as, "he was the one who sinned in the first place."

The church leadership is right in their estimation. The entire situation would not exist if the pastor had not sinned. The church would not be suffering if the pastor hadn't failed morally. Families would not have to explain to their children why the pastor had to leave. But it is also critical for churches to begin listening to the underlying cultural issues that may have led to the problem in the first place.

In this section, six major causes of social conflict have been identified as signals of the trap, precursors to a fall and hindrance to restoration: Isolation, poor relationship with the spouse, the original mistress, high expectations, judgmentalism, and the response to ministry failure. Seeing one of these symptoms in the life of a pastor is troublesome, but adding more than one may mean a call for intervention. Any of these factors can begin to brew and create a negative situation in the life of the pastor. So how can a fall be prevented? If the trap exists in the ministry culture, how can things change? How can temptation be recognized when one is weak? How can the church undergird the pastor and protect him?

Section Four

The Response

The question for the church is this: Can we take the risk to restore the pastor immediately? Can we step into the command to forgive and reveal a deeper sense of what the church is really about? As hard as that sounds, there is actually sound Biblical support for doing so.

When Peter denied following Jesus three times, Christ immediately sought him out and restored him, publicly. He immediately restored him to leadership, calling him to "feed my sheep." Peter's very public failure could never negate the call of God on his life, and Jesus knows this. Jesus' restoration reiterated Peter's direction and purpose for his life. And it was Jesus that made the first steps toward renewal. If Peter had not been restored, the church might not be where it is today.

As strange as it might sound to immediately restore someone to leadership, this is exactly what Jesus did. He called Peter right back to the same place he spent that last three years of his life, at the feet of Jesus, to follow, to learn and to grow. In restoring Peter, Jesus tests our bounds on grace and mercy. He pushes our buttons on what it means to really forgive. Could grace and mercy really extend that far?

Jesus had every right to be mad at Peter. He could have said, "What you did made me so angry. I hate what you did." But Jesus didn't. Instead he immediately stepped into a compassionate response. And in doing so he left behind the bitterness and resentment that could have possibly harmed him.

While Jesus' example is unique and Peter's sin was of a different machination than those in this book, it does provide us with a good beginning point for how forgiveness should proceed. Peter was restored. He wasn't cast aside. He wasn't judged harshly. Jesus didn't attempt to sweep the problem under the rug. He called it out and restored Peter.

Can churches get there immediately? Those instances are probably rare given the evidence in the previous stories. But it is possible.

Whether pastors will find restoration to the pulpit is a question that each person must answer for themselves. In fact, it will be argued that fallen pastors should not concentrate their efforts on pursuing ministry after their fall. Christ should be pursued first and foremost.

The restoration process is typically a long and arduous one. The pastor is in need of compassionate people who are willing to walk with him, show understanding and take a strong role in his life. In this final section, the stories that have been told and the facts that have been shared will be filtered into a hopeful way to help the fallen pastor.

It will begin with an intimate look with the time immediately after the pastor's fall. The pastor goes through a series of stages and those who are willing to help need to be prepared. Restoration will then be addressed with an eye toward what it takes to walk with the fallen pastor.

Preventing a fall will be addressed with the dual voices of Scripture and the pastors who fell. Finally, there must be a way to change the culture that is in place. Many operate within the culture unaware, pastors continue to fall and churches and ministry couples are weakened. Working together, the church community, pastors who serve, fallen ministers and those who desire to see change can reform the culture.

Chapter 18

Understanding The Common Patterns

Choosing to walk with a fallen pastor is a challenging but compassionate decision. The days and months immediately after his fall are filled with a wide range of emotions including shame, hurt, pride and anger. He is often quick to turn away help and ignore phone calls because he believes people are being insincere and he is unrepentant. However, it is a time in which he needs people to walk with him the most. In order for someone to do this, it is helpful to understand the common cycle that fallen pastors go through after their fall. If the pastor is to be restored, understanding his journey is necessary.

The stages of the post-fall can be categorized as: disorientation, increased pride, justification of sin, avoidance, shame, anger, increased sin, move toward brokenness, realization of sin, humility and desire toward restored relationships. Not all of these steps may take place and they may not take place in this exact order. These steps may take place over several months or over years. However, they do seem to be recurrent in each case and are cause for further examination.

Disorientation

When the pastor is first caught in his sin, he may or may not have been expecting it. Several of the pastors interviewed showed an inner desire to get caught. They wanted things to be over so the stress of hiding would be lessened. But once he gets caught and is confronted with his sin, he goes into the fight or flight mode.

It must be remembered that most fallen pastors have been living in a shadowy fantasy world up to the point of their discovery. They have been able to control the circumstances of their world, hiding their every move and controlling the information they share. At the moment their sin has been discovered, reality has struck. They may have had the belief that they were going to run off into the future with their lover with what they thought was a plan of genius. Reality is a harsh wake up call for those who have truly been immersed in fantasy. Dr. York reflected upon this:

> "Every time you have an affair with anybody, I don't care who you are, in a sense, you're having an affair with a fantasy and not a real person. Because the person you've got to pay the mortgage with, deal with the kids' soccer schedule with, the one whose vomit you wipe up when they're sick, that's the real person you live with. Twenty minutes in the sack on a Tuesday afternoon is really not love. You've got to tell yourself that. You've got to awaken yourself to the fact that it's fantasy. If you end up with the person you had an affair with, I guarantee you once you get married you have to face the same issues and same struggles. You cannot take two totally depraved human beings, stick them in the same house and not have friction."

Whether the fallen pastor truly intended on leaving his wife or continuing on in fantasy, he now faces the reality of a broken world around him including his deceived family members, church members, friends, children and his wife. He may suddenly be disoriented with the anger that surfaces from these people when they don't easily forgive him, reach out to him or even if they lash out at him in anger.

Increased Pride

After being separated from everything in his life because of sin, one might think the instinctive attitude for a Christian pastor would be humility. Unfortunately, the fallen minister has been living in a world of sin, external pressures and isolation for years and humility is not the easiest or most recognizable jumping off point for him. That is why close friends who are willing to walk with a broken minister are so necessary to guide him through this difficult process. David Trotter explained that his book was a guide to help people understand how difficult the fall is for a minister and the need for people to come alongside and help him repent:

> "It's not just a black and white issue of right or wrong, it's a very complex issue. I've told guys, 'You should stop,' but it's not such a black and white issue. It's a very complex issue. It's an insider's view of sin and brokenness and there should be some compassion for people and a willingness to walk with them."[48]

However, whether the pastor is ready to repent within a short, reasonable amount of time is the key for whether the hurt church should be willing to help the pastor in counseling. This does not necessarily mean the church is going to allow the preacher back into the pulpit, but the pastor who is in a true state of repentance is definitely one who is worth getting further help. In fact, the pastor who is ready to repent is showing a willingness to follow Christ and hopefully those who love Christ will receive his change of heart. Dr. York says a church has to be willing to help a pastor who has fallen into sin:

> "A church's posture has to be guided by whether or not there is repentance, because your posture has to be one thing if a person is living in defiance and embracing their sin. Then you have to confront. 1 Corinthians 5 kicks in and Paul describes as turning them over to Satan for the destruction of the flesh. There's nothing pretty about that. But if a person is broken and repentant over their sin, even if they want to be and they're not there yet, but they want to be. They may say, 'It's hard for me to leave this 23 year old girl who thinks I hung the moon and go back to a wife I struggled with for the past 20 years, but I want to do that because it honors the Lord.' Well, if a guy says that, then by all means, you've got to walk that walk with him, or see that someone does. Because sometimes the unity of the church matters too and the leaders in the church have to take care of the church but

what they cannot do is just abandon the one in sin and say,
'Well, you're on your own.'[49]

For fallen pastors, humility is difficult for many reasons. Josh stated that he wanted to work things out with Sue just to prove he hadn't thrown his marriage away for nothing. For Kris, like many other pastors, his ministry had been built on his pride. When his sin was discovered, pride wasn't something that he shed aside easily. Humbling circumstances are not the same as humility. People can have horrible events happen to them and equate them with humility, but they do not necessarily produce the attitude of humility God invites. Only a broken spirit before God can produce a right heart.

An example is that of Job, who after losing almost everything he had proclaimed before God, "The Lord gave and the Lord has taken away; blessed be the name of the Lord."[50] Unfortunately, many believe that a bad circumstance will automatically produce this type of humility. Another reason humility is difficult is because fallen pastors often do not see themselves as prideful. They begin to find reasons for the situations in which they find themselves and fault other people. The nights they spend alone begin to pile up and they dwell upon the circumstances that led them there begin to with. They may begin to blame stress at church, problems in their marriage or other reasons and feel justified in their actions.

Self-Justification

Self-justification is an exercise every Christian and non-Christian practices at one point. The fallen pastor has become proud and angry with those who continue to level accusations at him instead of engaging him with a loving response he believes he deserves. Many fallen pastors feel that the church should show more compassion and grace because of his years of service to them. In turn, he begins to justify his sin and may lash out in a passive aggressive manner or sin even further. In his mind, he finds ways to convince himself that all of his actions were right and in some cases, he may feel that he did no wrong. Some, like Gary, even use their theology to justify their actions:

"My theology didn't help me either. I embraced total depravity and that allowed me to justify some things."

Pastors who are in self-justification mode will not respond to those who come at them in anger, demanding they repent. The judgment seems to reinforce the pride as opposed to change it. However, this does not mean they should be abandoned. They still need friends who are willing to love them for who they are, yet confront them with compassion over their sin. They need genuine friends who will walk with them and listen when or if God eventually breaks their hearts over any sin in their life.

At some point, the fallen pastor will have to take responsibility for his actions, even if horrible circumstances were involved. Slowly, he will begin to understand that self-justification will only take him so far. Wilson noted that a good counselor or friend will aid in this process and show him that blaming others is a dead end road that only leads to more misery:

"Blaming others will bury you in an avalanche of self-righteousness and leave you to die at the bottom of the slope. It takes courage to face up to your sin and mistakes. It is a painful thing to let others see you as you really are. However, the other option is even more painful. If you refuse to accept blame, the reality of the situation does not change – not in God's eyes and not in the eyes of those who really know you. Blaming others robs you of the opportunity for confession, repentance, forgiveness and restoration to God and others."[51]

Shame and Avoidance

Understanding the shame that the fallen pastor feels is important for those who desire to walk in compassion with him. Shame is a form of internal judgment that devalues the inherent, God given worth of the individual. It comes about when guilt turns into self-judgment and the pastor reminds himself of former sin. Those who walk with the fallen pastor need to be aware that this feeling is very real and may last for a long time.

The shame he feels comes from his self-awareness of the hurt he has caused the church and as a result, he will avoid public places so as not to encounter those who would remind him of the pain he inflicted. He may also receive messages and reactions from family that let them know how disappointed they are. Some of the pastors interviewed dealt with terrible internalized shame that manifested itself physically. This is probably one of the worst periods of time for the fallen pastor and it lasts for months after the fall.

Gary said:

> "I was shamed and embarrassed in public, longing for forgiveness, wanting people to forgive me, to hear words of affirmation and forgiveness. I wanted to die. I remember praying, 'God kill me. Just don't let me wake up.'"

Denny said:

> "I lived in a large town and was well known. I would walk into a place and would feel like people were talking about me."

Lance said:

> "The first three months were so '9/11.' Everything I was and everything people thought I was gone. I got a voicemail from my dad who always thought I was the perfect child and he told me he didn't want to have anything to do with me. He disowned me."

Vincent said:

> "It was utter, physical revulsion. I had stomach and chest pain for weeks. Nausea. It was almost utter hopelessness."

Joe said:

> "It took four years to get back to a place where the pain wouldn't overwhelm me and the guilt and the shame."

Paul said:

> "I felt like a leper."

Dathan:

> *"My parents wouldn't have anything to do with me. It took seven years to mend fences with my dad and five or six for my mom."*

Shannon said:

> *"For me to tell you that it still doesn't hurt that I fell, I'd be telling a lie. I don't dwell on it. Maybe I haven't paid the price God wants me to pay yet. But I paid a price with my children and I paid a price with my friends."*

Josh said:

> *"I have church members who won't even look at me when I'm at Wal-Mart. That hurts. These are people who I was there when their families were hurting and they were grieving and when they made mistakes."*

Each of these feelings of shame are a result of the sin these men committed. Shame often occurs during the restoration process, especially when the pastor has not experienced brokenness. This is why restoration is vital, to help the fallen pastor move from shame to healing. Understanding the consequences of sin is a vital step, despite how difficult it is to see the pain in the faces of former church members. When Denny told his counselor he felt as if everyone was watching him, his counselor responded, "That's a big ego, to think they care that much about you." While this is true, the fallen pastor does receive negative public attraction and can internalize it more than necessary. What matters is his perception of those around him and his interaction with them. Before his healing continues, the pastor usually dives deeper into anger or increased sin.

Anger

With self-justification, pride, rejection by his former church and personal issues, the fallen minister often strides into a whirlwind of anger. Some lash out at their former churches for their reaction to their sin or the situation before the fall. Others are angry with their spouses for not providing them with sexual, emotional and spiritual needs. Some get angry with God for allowing them to fall or putting them in a position where they could fall. The anger they feel is another part of the blaming process, even though the people they find fault with may have contributed to the troubles that led them to the brink.

The anger that the pastor feels may come from the loss of relationships that are now severed. Many times, fallen pastors demand people forgive him when he utters an apology, even on the basis of Scripture. However, he does not realize that he has not reached a state of repentance. Wilson says that this is a bad sign:

> "Demanding forgiveness is often a sign of nonrepentance. The repentant heart longs for forgiveness but rests in the knowledge that the only guaranteed forgiveness comes from the heavenly Father."[52]

The pastor is angry at his church because the relationship is broken and he desires restoration. He becomes angry, knowing that Scripture calls for believers to forgive other believers and feels they have a Scriptural mandate to do so. It is a similar situation with his spouse. He may offer a lip-service apology with no true repentance and cannot understand why his wife won't forgive and it forms in him a deep, bitter anger. Worse, he then turns to God and cannot understand why God won't change the people's hearts and create forgiveness in them when what is needed most is humility from him and a change in his own heart.

Brokenness

In each of these cases, the men reached some level of brokenness. Many had been to counseling and understood the reasons for what they had done and had revealed character flaws within their life that had led them to sin. Most of the men reported it was God who had led them to a state of brokenness and humility as well as a significant set of circumstances. Typically, brokenness came after walking with people who were patient with them, intensive counseling and being involved in a church that cared about them.

Many fallen pastors seem to lose faith in the structure and work of the church. A cynical attitude sets in, especially after a bad experience in a conflicted church. Dominic made the observation that it is very difficult to get back into a church because:

> *"It's like working in the kitchen of a restaurant; you know everything that goes on back there."*

However, a church that is willing to help a pastor during his restorative process can aid him while he moves toward brokenness.

After his fall, Kris was welcomed into a fellowship that didn't ask him to do anything. He said:

> *"Every Sunday, we just showed up at that church and they loved on us."*

Lance had a similar experience as he connected to a church that he said:

> *"restored our faith in the institution of the church. They were interested in us as people."*

Despite the fact that this church wasn't responsible for their restoration, they sent Lance and Kari to a ministry restoration center for intensive treatment. Undoubtedly, a church that is willing to love a fallen pastor instead of allowing him to sit on the back pew can make a life-changing difference as God begins to bring brokenness into his world.

Hershael York has dealt with many fallen ministers and recognizes when a pastor is truly broken over his sin. He recalled one young pastor he was counseling who was recalling the events of his adultery. The young pastor still had a slight smirk on his face when he recalled his sin. Dr. York said:

> *"He didn't hate his sin yet. He was still in a place where that sin was still delicious to him. I told him, 'It's terrible that I'm more broken over your sin than you are.'"*[53]

Brokenness is only possible when the man reaches a deeper sense of true repentance toward God. For the fallen pastor still caught up in "the deliciousness of sin," it may be difficult to understand the difference between a simple apology and biblical repentance. Most pastors are aware of the biblical definition of repentance – a complete turning away from sin. However, when fallen ministers are in the process of self-justification, they may need help understanding what constitutes a more practical repentance in their situation. Earl Wilson, who suffered ministry failure, wrote that a mere apology is insufficient:

> "Apologies are difficult because to apologize requires that I admit that I have done something wrong. When most people apologize, they do so without admitting their error. They just offer a quick 'Sorry' as an apology. It is easier to say 'Sorry' than to say, 'I was wrong.'"[54]

When pastors begin to take ownership of their sin and understand their transgression before God, they move toward humility. When pastors can begin to understand that repentance is a continual action and moving away from sin, they can begin to heal. Again, Wilson states:

> "I teach men to understand their repentance by using the phrase, 'That's no longer an option for me.'"[55]

There eventually comes a time when a pastor comes full circle in his brokenness. It is probably the most important time for the fallen pastor in the restoration process. Dr. York gave two characteristics of a pastor who has been completely broken. He calls it "The March of Brokenness":

> "A man cannot be restored until he's broken over his sin and not just the consequences of his sin."[56]

He claims for the fallen pastor that there is a sense in which he will never get past the mark of his sin. However, he also stated:

> "What you have to do is make sure that your repentance becomes more notorious than your sin, so that when this is whispered about you, someone says, 'that is just so hard to believe.'"[57]

He said when he sees the following two characteristics of brokenness in a man's life, he knows that he has moved toward restoration. The first mark of brokenness is when a pastor realizes he doesn't get to judge someone's reaction to his sin:

"If you're genuinely broken to your sin, you realize the people who are all handling it wrong were put in that position because you sinned; you had the choice, they didn't."[58]

Fallen pastors have the tendency to become angry when they hear outpourings of hatred and anger from their former church leadership, church members or family. It sparks within them an equal reaction of anger and sometimes a negative response. However, Dr. York says this is not a reaction of brokenness, but of pride:

"They're still wrong [in their sinful reaction], someone needs to go up and correct them but the guy who is in sin can't do it."[59]

He shared that the angry person may be responding with improper levels of hatred, but that is not the pastor's concern. The pastor needs to show humility since he began the wheel of emotion turning.

This characteristic deals with the minister taking responsibility for his sin. His sin has triggered an amazing outpouring of emotions across the community that he cannot control and should not try to control. For a long time, the best the fallen pastor can do is wait in patience and humility. When he does come to a place of repentance, he may offer apology, however, the worst thing he can do is offer justification for what he did or respond in anger to those who are bitter toward him. The pastor cannot always expect forgiveness immediately, if ever. Dr. York said:

"When I see a guy who is bitter and angry at somebody's response to his sin, I realize he's not completely there yet. He has to have a complete accepting of responsibility for his sin. Their sin is their sin. I'm not justifying a bad reaction, that's sin too. But it's the same way a fallen pastor might say, 'Me and my wife didn't have sex for years.' I might say, 'There's no question she set you up for failure according to 1 Corinthians 7:10. But the same Bible teaches that doesn't give you an excuse to go sin. You've got to accept responsibility for your sin and you can't be angry with her.'"[60]

The other mark of brokenness Dr. York recognizes is "The Prodigal Son Response."

> "It is a total lack of entitlement."[61]

When the prodigal son returned from leaving home, he came back to his father and told him he wasn't worthy of working for him and begged to work as one of his hired hands. Dr. York said that was where a fallen pastor needs to be in his state of brokenness:

> "When a man gets there then I really have no doubt God can still use him and he'll get back to where he needs to be. It's when you love others and enemies like you want them to love you."[62]

Fitting In

Like most people, a pastor's identity is wrapped up in his vocation. Unlike most, the pastor was called specifically by God to a lifetime of church vocation. The loss of his ministry is devastating and trying to become "just a church member" is often a humbling and harrowing experience. Some fallen pastors avoid church for a long time, attempting to avoid the pain of the remembrances that come to them when they enter a place of worship. Some stay away due to continued sin. Some find it difficult to "ride the pine" after being behind the pulpit for so long. Being in the place of leadership and preaching the Word of God is a difficult thing for a minister to relinquish, even if it was by his own hand and sinful decision.

Despite these issues, the fallen minister must find a community of faith to link to that will help restore his soul, and if necessary, rebuild his faith. All of the experts consulted for this work expressed the same thought – recovery is a process of years, not months. Any pastor who desires any sort of restoration needs to cultivate patience and be ready to listen to the opinions of those he has set over him as mentors. In a way, this patience will draw the fallen pastor to a closer walk with God. Several of the ministers interviewed called this their time of "wilderness wandering" much like the Israelites wandered seeking God's eventual home for them. Mark Roberts shared his views of restoration:

"I know there are some Christians who think restoration should never happen and there are others who think if you stand up and just say you're sorry you should be immediately restored as if forgiveness is just authorization for ministry. I don't think that's the case. I've seen things that really impress me as being biblical and wise. It's always an extended time away from the immediate pastoral ministry. There's always a context for real growth emotionally, psychologically, spiritually, really helping pastors get at what's going on in their lives and that takes time. It's more than a couple of months, we're talking many months or years and with accountability with people who can help discern."[63]

When a pastor reaches a point of brokenness it is common that opportunities arise for him to speak about the process, to speak into other communities about the grace and mercy that is possible in a community and in a soul. The pastor who has found grace has found the most valuable thing of all. He has found Jesus Himself and He is worth sharing. He has found the compassionate Savior who reached out to him when no one else would. It is Christ who spurns us on to replicate His love so that we might multiply His work so many more might see what He can do.

Summary

Despite the fact that he has called down consequences upon himself, the fallen pastor is in need of having understanding people to walk with him through a difficult time. It is a time where he will question his salvation, become angry with God, reject help from well meaning individuals and possibly sink deeper into sin. He will be openly criticized, publicly ridiculed and turn from idol to idiot overnight. Those who do choose to walk with him and show him patience, love and care run the risk of being scorned by their peers. Christians are called to walk alongside one another, seeking to restore one another when they fall. It should always be clear that those who walk with the fallen pastor are not affirming his sin, but loving him as a child of God.

Chapter 19

Restoring The Fallen

Churches are now being faced with a great challenge. How do we change the culture that leads to the problem, but also how do we deal with the men who have already fallen? If the church cannot restore the pastor when he falls, who can we restore? If grace and mercy mean anything to the church, shouldn't it begin with its leader?

When a pastor falls, it is an event that triggers a strong emotional reaction throughout the community, regardless of belief. Some are compassionate, some are angry but most are confused by the actions of one who called himself a man of God. When a well-known pastor is scandalized, the media push is intensified as public opinion is heaped on that man's shoulders.

In the previous section, four reasons for weakness were identified for a pastor before his fall. With the pastors interviewed, each of them felt weak in at least three of the four areas. There appeared to be a moment where each of them "broke" and, upon looking back, realized they were weak. Shannon said he knew better and yet proceeded forward. He called it the "point of no return." Kris felt it when Karla came into his office and began to tell him about her marriage problems. He called it "that defining moment where you look back." The well of sexual temptation is open to these men where it seemingly wasn't even a consideration before. Dominic called it the moment when "the doors opened."

Most often, the minister discovers someone on their staff, within their church or a close family friend who has a sympathetic ear. It should be noted that in each case, the pastor wasn't searching for a companion and most often, neither was the person they encountered. Several pastors used the terminology that they "clicked" with the person they discovered. Each relationship began as an emotional relationship. The minister, who was most often emotionally needy, fed on this relationship and was nourished by a new appreciation for who he was, meeting his perceived need. For the rest of his life, the adulterous pastor will live with the scarlet letter emblazoned upon his chest, enduring looks of pity, scorn, anger and pretentious looks from other pastors as his years pass by.

Scripture calls upon us to restore those who sin. It means walking together with him until the shattered pieces of his soul are restored and his walk with Christ is renewed. There are many issues that need to be addressed before, during and after his restoration. In order to do this, the pastor must find friends willing to walk with him to help and restore him. Many of the ministers interviewed said their church was ill equipped to help them after their fall and reacted harshly.

Gary's story is a solid example of how a community of faith should respond to the fallen pastor. The church leadership reacted quickly to reach out to him, even when they were disillusioned and hurt. Spiritual leaders in the community worked with him for months through his sin as he sought repentance and reconciliation with his wife. It is a difficult process, but one that is absolutely necessary to restore those who have fallen.

Unfortunately, most responses offered by the church culture today toward the fallen pastor are insufficient if we are to move toward changing the culture. There are only two places we can be in this battle to change the way things are, and they mirror the reactions of the people in the story of the adulterous woman. One group stands aside judging, ready to cast stones or ready for a verdict to be rendered. The other response is one of compassion, being ready to show compassion. This response requires patience, understanding and a readiness to be separate from the majority. Jesus restored the woman caught in adultery immediately. He did not dismiss her sin, but neither did he condemn her. He looked past the picture that the crowd had painted and saw her as an imperfect person who needed love, compassion and a friend.

Earl Wilson noted three typical reactions of the church when a pastor falls.[64] The first is one he calls "cheap grace" where the pastor is allowed to quickly apologize and possibly enter a brief time of counseling. The pastor does not enter a true period of repentance and no true restoration is seen. The second response is a legalistic one where the pastor is removed from the church: "Little thought is given to restoration of the individual to fellowship with God or the church family. And the recovery of the spouse and family members is ignored."[65] The final response is when the church completely ignores the issue and attempts to cover it up. Wilson claims this is the most common response. However, in each of the respondents to this study, the legalistic approach was the most common and only one pastor was offered counseling.

Sexual sin is probably judged the harshest in our communities of faith. Even in those times, it calls upon fellowships to look upon Christ for the answer for finding compassion and forgiveness. Dr. York commented on the need for understanding in this area:

> "I know we categorize sins and make like some are worse than others and I know for certain consequences that's true. But for not for the death of Christ, it doesn't matter what sin you've committed, it required His atoning sacrifice as much as any other."[66]

Pastor and counselor Roger Barrier said that the legalistic approach should be expected and the pastor should not expect his former church to restore him due to the pain he has caused them:

> "When a pastor commits adultery the trust is so deeply blown that it would take years to restore the trust. It's like when you commit adultery, what's gone with your wife? The trust. It just takes a long time to build the trust. The fallen pastor has to get his expectations in line with reality. You don't walk through your recovery alone. You have to have some vulnerable friends who will walk through it with you. The fallen pastor has to find another source for healing. It will not be the church forgiving him. It will be the friends he cultivates walking him through the process."[67]

Barrier mentioned one of the most important aspects of the restoration process that needs to be addressed in the beginning. The fallen pastor has lost the trust of many people. During the time of his affair, the pastor spent a length of time deceiving his friends, family, church and spouse in order to hide his adultery. After being discovered, it will be very difficult for the fallen pastor to restore trust with those close to him again. In some ways, the breaking of the trust may have been a more serious sin to some than the pastor's sin of adultery. The pastor cannot expect immediate results in this area, whether with his spouse or with his colleagues. This is why finding the right help in restoration is necessary.

Wilson, et. al., have done the most comprehensive work on the subject of restoration. They recommend a team of people who are willing to give up large amounts of time and love for the pastor in peril. Restoration is not an easy or short termed process and those who are willing to undertake it are in for a serious, heart wrenching time. The following characteristics and approaches are vital:

> "Restoration is neither accidental nor automatic. It requires deliberate involvement. Friends around the hurting individual can help best by (1) listening kindly, (2) acknowledging the seriousness of the situation rather than assisting in the destructiveness of denial, and (3) urging the fallen person to look for help so the move toward restoration can begin."[68]

Restoration is also of the utmost importance because it is the healing of the relationship between the fallen minister and God. Several of the respondents said that they had been more involved with ministry than in a relationship with Christ. When asked about restoration, Joe said:

> "There are so many men who want to be restored to ministry but they miss the whole point of being restored back to the Lord."

When David fell with Bathsheba, he proclaimed to God, "Against you, you only, have I sinned and done what is evil in your sight."[69] The pastor has hurt many people, harmed many relationships, but the account of his sin

How To Help A Fallen Pastor

Avoid the cliché: If he asks, "Why did this happen?" Don't respond with statement like, "It was God's will," or "This too shall pass." He's probably heard it all. Respond with meaningful things, "I don't know, but I'm sorry you're hurting and I'm here to help you." Or just, "I don't know, but I love you and I don't judge you and I'll do whatever I can to help."

Don't view him differently: He's the same person he was before. Just because he sinned doesn't make him a different man. He hasn't become a leper or the worst person in the community. He's still the same, weak person he was before.

Just be there: One day, when the darkness begins to fade away, he'll remember a very important thing – the people who stood by him when he was at his lowest. It may not seem like much to you, but you're ministering and saving a man's life.

Take him out to lunch, just because: Surprise him by taking him out and don't bring up anything about his fall. If he wants to talk about it, let him. If you're counseling him, walk with him through it. But don't press the issue all the time. Just remember to be friends once in a while.

Remember to call him, especially on days when you really don't want to: Fallen pastors who just fell have some very sad thoughts. Don't leave him to his thoughts, especially on his bad days. Let him know you care with a quick phone call, email, text or visit.

Network with other fallen pastors: Find people who have been through what he's been through and might be willing to talk to him about their restorative experience. There is a list of books in the bibliography he might find helpful to read as well.

Never let him forget the love of God: He probably feels like everyone, including God hates him. One thing you can remind him of is the amazing love of Christ and how He loves us despite of our sin. Remind him of Psalm 103 or Psalm 23. Read them together with him or write them down personally and send them in a card.

is to God. That relationship must be restored and made right if all else is to be restored. When finding friends and counsel to aid him in restoration, the pastor must find wise, godly people to help him in his walk. If he neglects his broken relationship with God, he may fall further than he already has:

> *"The foundation for restoration is reconciliation with God. It begins with God's working in the heart of the one whose choices have led him or her into sin and separation from God. God wants to be in relationship with his children. The restoree loses sight of this truth and often believes that God has no use for him or her. For someone to desire restoration, he or she needs a renewed view of God's mercy and his demand for personal holiness."* [70]

Denny has had the chance to help many other ministers since his fall. He recommended men find the right kind of counselor during the restoration process:

> *"There are counselors out there and there are good counselors."*

The fallen minister should take care to find someone who understands his plight emotionally, spiritually and socially. Earl Wilson reflected that sentiment in his book:

> *"Select a therapist who understands your specific problem. The role of the therapist is to be a careful observer and to help restorees squarely face their issues. The more the therapist understands the problem, the greater the likelihood that a restoree will be helped to face his or her issues in ways that will lead to positive outcomes. A therapist, Christian or non-Christian, will not be helpful unless he or she has enough awareness of the problem to help the restoree face the key issues."* [71]

Choosing to Walk With the Fallen Pastor

Taking on the task of loving a fallen pastor is not an easy decision. It means standing against the roar of those who judge, but it also means standing with Christ. It means putting aside a judgmental attitude and stooping down to understand the depths to which the pastor has fallen. It means listening when he needs someone to listen and giving sound, biblical advice when he needs it. Most of all, it requires a heart that simply loves him for the man God created him to be and being a friend when all else have seemingly rejected him for his sin.

But to engage the fallen it must be clearly stated: Standing with those who have fallen does not validate what the person has done. If this were true, even Jesus would be in trouble. Standing with the fallen means holding onto their dignity as a human being regardless of their actions. Is it easy? No. But does it create a better situation long-term? Yes.

There is a kind of "guilty by association" attitude against fallen pastors that seems to be common. As soon as a pastor falls, many people abandon his side and cannot put enough space between themselves and him. If one chooses to walk with a fallen pastor, they might be perceived to be in this situation. It is a difficult stigma to battle with and some never overcome it enough to approach the fallen pastor.

The opposite reaction can be seen in Christ who went out of his way to identify with the sinners who no one else wanted to talk to. He loved the unlovable and broke many societal trends of his day. In doing so, he showed us a new way to love and showed His followers what to expect if they wanted to be like Him.

The stories of fallen pastors are rife with rejection of those outside the church.

Kris said:

> "It's funny because you lose all your friends, your pastor friends want nothing to do with you, you find out they're really not your friends."

Denny said:

> "Only a handful of people contacted me or supported me and none of them were in the ministry. All of them said the

> *same thing to me, 'We don't care, you're still Denny. Nothing*
> *has changed.'"*

Dathan said:

> *"Most of my friends in the ministry would have nothing to*
> *do with me except for two. They said, 'You're done, buddy.*
> *To have anything to do with me would be to condone my*
> *actions."*

The stories of rejection can be viewed in two ways. There is a period of time in which fallen pastors seem to reject any phone calls or contact from anyone who calls because of their shame or situation. Some well-meaning pastors, friends and church leaders attempt to call, but often, the fallen pastor questions their motives. In my case, I didn't answer the phone when at least two local pastors called right after my fall. It was because I didn't want to talk to them, it was because of the shame I felt.

It is a difficult thing for many in the community who once identified and associated with the pastor to surround him after his sin. There appears to be a "guilty by association" relationship between former friends and pastors as he finds himself without support or help. The angst that some feel is due to not knowing what to say. Others may simply want to wash their hands of their former relationship.

In Luke 15, Christ related the parable of the lost sheep. A shepherd had 100 sheep and one went astray. The shepherd left the entire flock to search after the one that was lost. When he found that sheep, he was overjoyed, reflecting the joy we have over the one sinner who repents in contrast to the 99 who do not need to repent. Similarly, when a brother or sister in Christ falls, the flock is incomplete without them. Seeking them out tirelessly and compassionately as the shepherd did is a responsibility for the health of the church.

When fallen pastors hit rock bottom with no help from friends willing to walk with them, they often continue to spiral downward. After his fall, Josh said:

> *"I was at that point I didn't think I had anything to lose. I had lost my family, lost my job, my reputation was already marred, what more could happen?"*

This time could be called a time of extreme despair for the fallen pastor as he may see no way out of his situation, but walking with the fallen pastor may be one of the most redeeming choices a person can make. Some pastors may view it as the end of the useful portion of their lives. That attitude can be changed if people surround the fallen pastor, willing to walk with him through difficult times and show him the same compassion as Christ.

Chapter 20

Preventing The Fall

If we could watch the fall of the pastor on video and watch it backward in slow motion, we would see him move from downward to upward. We would witness him going from sin to righteousness, from fallen to adored pastor on a pedestal. If we were able to witness his fall in reverse slow motion, we would also see him go from being isolated to being surrounded by a community of faith. We would suddenly understand that the fall of the pastor happens within a certain church culture that breeds a trap.

It is a culture that has been in place in our churches for decades and like many of our unquestioned traditions, it has reproduced itself unknowingly, but it keeps breeding the same type of pattern. It lays traps for pastors, placing them high upon a pedestal to only see them willingly accept the place of an idol then fall alone into the pit.

This culture is so entrenched into the mind of the church member that it is unquestioned. It has taken the place of compassion and forgiveness for those who fall into sin. Instead of offering restoration, it lashes out in anger and judgment. It is not a culture that was envisioned by the early church or by the Christ who stood by the adulterous woman in John 8.

It is a culture that unwittingly seeks out to destroy. It is a culture that has blinded many of us for years without our knowledge and unfortunately can only be exposed to some by a fall of their own as they are shown the need for forgiveness. It is, though, a culture that can be redeemed by the true community of faith and message of love that Christ originally brought to his people.

If this culture is to be broken and if fallen pastors are to be restored, it will be done by a community that understands that all have sinned and fall short of the glory of God. It will be done by a community that understands that in the story of John 8, the angry mob that puts down their rocks is a mob that suddenly realizes they are no better off than the woman at the feet of Jesus. In fact, the adulterous woman who found herself at the feet of Christ was the richest woman in the world at that moment. Despite her sin and what seemed to be an imminent death sentence, she had found a best friend for life and a message that gave her life everlasting. She had been set free from condemnation and judgment.

The true community of faith starts at the feet of Christ, focused upon Him. It begins by understanding the Savior and how far He has redeemed each of us. In God's community, we have all been rescued from the angry, accusing mob. Each of us was worthy of a stoning, but we were rescued and saved by Jesus. He stood in our place and now we stand together, equal. All ground is level at the foot of the cross.

Looking forward, none of us is immune from a future fall. It will happen that one of us in this humble community of faith will have a great fall. When that happens, a quick reminder of grace should come flooding to our minds of how much we have been forgiven. Christ forgave us much and loved us. How much more should we be ready to love and reach out to those within our community who fall?

The moment we refuse to restore and we begin to judge is the same moment we leave the side of our Master and run to join the crowd and pick up our stones, ready to cast them at the one who is fallen. As we aim our stones, we must remember that Christ is directly beside that person, not condoning their sin, but showing compassion.

What specific steps can a loving Christian community take alongside a pastor to prevent setting the trap and to reform the culture that currently exists? Avoiding ministry failure, like restoration, involves a team that is intentionally involved and aware of the issues as well as the entire church caring for the soul of the pastor. The pastor must know of the traps that exist and be ready to educate his church to join him in a quest to authentic community. He must also include his wife, friends, church and God in a prevention program if he wants to be serious about preventing ministry failure.

Build Authentic Relationships

The first step to avoiding ministry failure is to build authentic relationships. The pastor must be able to find people around him he can trust to share his weaknesses and struggles with. He must also be ready to share the joy of authentic Christian community with his church, allowing them to come alongside him to counter his weaknesses and be patient with him in his struggles. Both the pastor and church must also be ready to avoid the trap of allowing the pastor to view success as a launching point for becoming an idol in the eyes of himself, the congregation or the community.

Personal accountability is also a definite must for the pastor, but simply having an accountability partner may not be enough. Troy Haas stressed the importance of something more than accountability partner:

> *"I would advocate for something beyond accountability. We all know guys who were in accountability relationships but they were just lying to their accountability partners."*[72]

He stresses that the pastor needs to be able to open up and be himself with someone and be authentic. Many pastors find themselves overwhelmed with the duties of the pastorate and find little time to cultivate real relationships. If the pastor is already in a situation where he is viewed as an idol, he must find a way to climb down from the pedestal the congregation has set up for him and be human. Opening himself up to someone in an authentic accountability relationship about his weaknesses, struggles and vulnerability is an excellent way to begin. Haas says the pastor must be intentional about forming these relationships:

> *"He's got to find someone in his community. He can't be satisfied with those obstacles keeping him from that. I would say that he would be a more effective pastor if he could be more real with his congregation. While I know that's scary and he may have been hurt before, I think the benefits far outweigh the dangers in finding a small group*

of trustworthy folks. The reality is community is dangerous
no matter who you are or where you're doing it."[73]

Being accountable is a difficult thing for most people, not just pastors. To be truly accountable and to build a meaningful relationship takes time and energy. It is the pattern we see with Christ and His disciples. Throughout the gospels, we see their faults exposed, but we also see them growing in sanctification. The pastor is in dire need of discipling just as much as the church member. Many pastors resist authentic relationships because they know of their own hidden sins and faults and resist exposure.

Some pastors may make the mistake of feeling that being in the role of pastor is enough to keep them away from sin. They may feel that their sermon preparation, visitation and other duties may keep them invulnerable to temptation. The problem occurs when the pastor begins to fall into sin and actually uses the ministry as a penance of sorts:

> *"For many, their spiritual status gave them a sense of feeling*
> *moral and good. When the guilt or shame over their secret*
> *sexual lives bothered them, they could escape to their*
> *spiritual spaces and receive reinforcement that they were*
> *good men."[74]*

But imagine, for a moment, the freedom from sin when having an authentic relationship. As soon as sin crosses the mind of a pastor, he can call or contact his close friend without fear of judgment or exposure. The confession of the mere thought of sin has the effect of diffusing the sin and bringing it to the light so it may be dealt with. This type of relationship might be sought with a local pastor who is older and willing to mentor, a counselor, a wise deacon from another church or a director of missions.

Throughout the research done for this book, it has been suggested that pastors find it difficult to confide in their church leadership. Many pastors are distrustful of leadership or are unwilling to get close enough to church leaders to confide in them. After the fall, pastors find themselves with a self-fulfilling prophecy when their church leaders turn on them and without compassion, send them quickly out of the church. But what if the church culture were to change?

In the early church, we find a community that desperately depended upon one another for all things. In fact, without one another, they could not have functioned. It was them against the ruling powers of the day. There seems to be an inherent distrust between many pastors and leadership, but that is not a biblical model. It is a symptom of a problem within a sick culture.

A community of authentic compassion and trust, understanding one another's weaknesses and faults, centered on Christ would not have a pattern of distrust. Instead, a pastor could have a team of leaders to whom he could confide in and share his problems with. The leaders could also share their problems equally with confidence. How can this occur?

It can only occur when a change happens from within each person, focused upon a common goal. When each person understands that the church is not made up of individual members but a community struggling together – a community that does not feel better or higher than anyone else, but strives to remember that each is like the woman cast at the side of Christ. True, Christian community can only come from a desire from each member to remember that none within the group is greater – certainly not the pastor – but each person is valued equally in the eyes of Christ.

Pursue Your Wife

Without exception, each of the ministers interviewed had either a terrible or slack relationship with their spouse. Their relationship worsened the longer they stayed in the ministry. Some complained that they were not able to share their problems at church with their wife or that communication did not exist. Several said that sexual intimacy had not taken place for a long time and their relationship had struggled severely because of it. Each of the men stated that they had communication or intimacy issues for years but never considered looking for a chance to commit adultery. Eventually with the other stressors that surrounded them, they eventually gave into sin. Wilson noted one of the most common ways that sin infiltrated the mind of the pastor:

> *"Research has shown that most sexual affairs start with inappropriate opening up of one's personal life to someone other than one's spouse. People long for honest sharing*

and to be heard and responded to by others. Inappropriate self-disclosure creates an intimacy or possibly a false intimacy, and this leads to a neglect of marital intimacy while emotional investments are made in relationships that threaten the marriage."[75]

The problem often begins when the pastor begins to pursue the ministry rather than his wife. He finds more satisfaction in his relationship with the mistress of the ministry than he does with his spouse. The ministry can give him higher levels of appreciation and acceptance than she can and it comes as a rush to his system and as time goes on, he needs more and more. Unfortunately, the ministry he chases after is a ministry based on success and the pleasing of people. It is a false system that is placing him on a pedestal and unwittingly setting him up for ministry failure. While he pursues it, those trapped in the culture are unaware of the trap being set and the pastor truly believes he is doing the work of God.

In many of the interviews, pastors found themselves in a Catch-22 situation. They were in marriage that they no longer wanted to be in, but they knew if they divorced, they would lose the ministry. Most of these men felt this way before they ever entered into a relationship outside their marriage. This troublesome symptom is another sign of the broken culture. Pastors are willing to stay in a relationship they feel is beyond redemption to chase after a system that fulfills their needs of admiration and appreciation. The system itself does nothing to help their marriage, in fact, it may be partially responsible for the deterioration of it. The pastor feels trapped, knowing that if he leaves his marriage, which he chased after for the expense of the culture, he will no longer have the platform where he finds fulfillment. This is a cycle that must be broken if pastors and their spouses are to find future hope.

The greatest thing that can happen to help ministry marriages is to change the broken culture. One of the most interesting findings in the interviews were the number of pastors who said their wives never "bought into" the ministry. Some of them had fathers or relatives who had seen the bad side of ministry and did not want to go through it. The spouse eventually relinquished and entered the ministry, typically with a resistant attitude.

Could it be that the ministry spouse was somewhat aware of the traps that lie ahead in the ministry culture? Might they have been attempting on some level to protect their husbands and families from future failure?

Once again, to reform the culture, a heart level change must occur. The pastor must first find his passion and acceptance at home with his wife instead of chasing the mistress of ministry. He must reiterate to himself on a constant basis that his wife and family love him and that his love for them should be a different kind of love than he has for the church. He must deliberately place priority over his spouse, cherish her and love her and not forsake her in the pursuit of any earthly passion. He must love her in the manner of the poetry found in the Song of Solomon. This kind of love is commanded of a husband in the book of Ephesians, to love a wife like Christ loved the church and gave Himself up for her.[76] A self-sacrificing love that exceeds all else, putting all others aside.

If a pastor does this, he can affect the culture immediately. He will set an example for the culture in which he lives. He will set an example for his children. More importantly, he will communicate to his wife through his actions and words that she is more important to him than chasing after any passion, success or admiration from anything or anyone else.

If a church wishes to aid the ministry couple, they can do several things. As previously mentioned, the pastor cannot be placed on a pedestal. Similarly, the pastor's wife cannot be exalted either. She is a human being, prone to faults, personality problems and occasional bad days like anyone else. They are not a perfect couple. They argue, quarrel and have real world problems. They have financial problems, their kids talk back and some Sundays, they want to take a vacation from church too. The community of faith can respect the ministry couple's boundaries and personal time at home, allow them to be human and ask them if they have any needs.

Even better, the community of faith can view them not as estranged people, but as friends, inviting them to share in their personal lives, struggles and homes. True Christian community lasts longer than two hours on Sunday. It extends all week and does not end at the door of the church foyer. Christian community is constantly on the minds of the people, lifting one another up in prayer, communicating with one another constantly and picking the other up when they fall.

Unfortunately, the culture will not change overnight. There are many pastors and their spouses who are currently struggling in their roles. Even if the culture does change, it does not guarantee that there will cease to be problems.

Many congregations would be shocked to discover that their pastor and his wife were not emotionally or sexually intimate. As the statistics at the beginning of this book indicate, it is a relatively common occurrence. Bill Leonard stated that pastors are often the last people to consider counseling and feel they can mend themselves, but he said that was like a doctor attempting to perform surgery on himself.[77]

What can be done for pastors to prevent the specific problems that plague ministry marriages? Too often, a band-aid approach is suggested for a bleeding wound. A pastor and his wife are sent away for a weekend retreat when what is needed is an intensive restorative process. The problem is not that the pastor and his wife need to be restored to one another. The problem lies in the culture that they have been introduced to. Unless the pastor and his wife can identify and understand the culture, they will continue to have problems. Unless the church culture itself changes, ministry marriages will continue to fail.

It cannot be emphasized enough that a pastor must treasure and protect his relationship with his wife. If marital counseling is needed, then it should be pursued. If a lengthy break from the pulpit could help the pastor and his wife grow closer together and heal their marriage, then it should be done. Dr. York gave the following advice:

> "You have to pursue your wife too. There is a courtship, a dance of seduction. My wife and I have tried our dead best to get the same kind of thrill that people seek in affairs. I've watched people have affairs and how much time and money it cost them and thought, 'If they had spent that much energy and money in their marriage as they did in their affair, they'd have a better marriage.'"[78]

Throughout the study, pastors said their wives were unwilling to listen to their problems at church. There must be a way in which a pastor and his spouse can communicate effectively about the ministry, which consumes their lives on a daily basis. It is the all-consuming culture in which they live. As Dominic described it, it is the "fishbowl." There is no blame to be cast in either direction, to be sure. But the weight of ministry does come across the threshold of the parsonage each evening and the pastor has a need to share the joys and worries of it with his wife.

Jim Simmons, my mentor in the faith, likened marriage communication to a radio receiver. A message is being broadcast and in order for it to be received, there must be a willing and operating vessel to hear what is being said. Communication has never been easy for humans, much less in marriage. Like other couples, ministry couples have not been instructed sufficiently on how to communicate with one another. Add on top of that the extreme stress of the pastorate and communication often becomes shut off. David Trotter, after his fall, shared some insights on how he and his wife worked to improved communication:

> *"The biggest challenge for me is that all my energy was going into the church. There was such a vacuum inside my soul and ego that needed to be filled and the thought of really making my wife and kids the huge priority of my life as us being partners; that's probably the key word that my wife and I processed a lot was that we needed to be a partner with one another. We were not partners before and now we're better partners than ever. For me, it's all about developing a partnership with my wife. And whenever that partnership begins to wane, I have a heads up that we're not quite connecting."*[79]

While living unaware in the fishbowl culture, the pastor and his wife often have two different views on the church. The spouse may see a kind group of people who are kind to her children and hold her in high esteem. The pastor, on the other hand, deals with business, marriage conflicts, counseling, visitation and often sees the dark underbelly of the church. When he arrives home, he may complain about certain people and his view is contrary to what the wife has viewed. The pastor may complain too much and if he does, his wife may begin to tune him out or deny his communication altogether. Even if his complaints are valid, he may be expressing only negative statements, isolating his wife, who may have positive views of the church. If their views continue to separate, communication may become completely severed.

The ministry couple may need to seek counseling on how to listen to one another. They must work together and equally on their relationship. It is important to constantly pray together, listen to one another's pain, understand the other's faults and be willing to listen about problems in the church even if one doesn't see it from a certain perspective. It was said before that the pastor could benefit from being vulnerable in front of his church and sharing his weakness. Even more important is that he remain vulnerable to his wife and her acceptance of his vulnerabilities. Pastor Mark Roberts shared the need for a constant reexamination of the ministry marriage:

> *"To be the wife of a pastor is a challenging thing. The wife often gets caught up in the expectations of the church. Pastoring can be a demanding, most certainly emotionally. It takes you out at strange times, you rarely get a normal weekend as a family where you can just be together. It's just so easy for pastors and pastor's wives to not pay attention to what's going on in the marriage. That opens up a window of vulnerability for relational and sexual temptations. The challenge is for pastors and their wives to really look at their lives and the challenges that are entering into it and ask, 'Am I building a strong marriage that is going to last? Am I taking my future for granted and letting it slowly weaken or die off? Am I getting to the place where my marriage is not meeting my emotional needs such that I'm vulnerable to some other person coming in so they can meet those needs?'"[80]*

The pastor must also understand that his wife is more than a church member and he cannot treat her like a routine visit, speaking in generalities and small talk. It seems to be a pattern for some pastors that the ministry begins to take precedence over everything in their lives, including their devotional time, their love of God, their family and even their spouse. The pastor must appreciate his spouse's needs and feelings as much as he expects her to appreciate his. She may feel small in comparison to him or his work.

Pastor's wives often give up their careers or dreams to raise families and feel just as underappreciated as the pastor, if not more. It's possible that the ministry spouse has been "waiting in line" all day to tell her husband something very important when he arrives home, only to find him preoccupied with the business of church. When ministry becomes more important than their spouse, the relationship will falter and communication will cease, leading down a dangerous path.

Ministry couples must strive even harder than most couples to make a marriage work. The husband is called upon to love his wife as Christ loves the church and the wife is asked to follow his leadership. In the midst of that, throw in the high demand of ministry, outside conflict and even the positives of church growth and success in evangelism. Each of these things will create stress upon a marriage which is why communication is vital every day for the ministry couple. The communication must be horizontal, between the two, being productive with active listening and use words that communicate clearly and positively. The ministry couple must also come together and communicate vertically with God in prayer.

A common complaint from pastors is, "I don't get to worship with my wife. Each Sunday, I'm preaching and I miss getting to sit with her and have my arm around her." The ministry couple must find ways to express worship to God together and fill this void, whether it is in the quiet of their home, with other ministry couples or as a family. The pastor and his wife must seek to have their souls rested and restored by God on a regular basis because the regular demands of ministry will drain them often.

Ministry couples should never cease to rediscover their first love for one another. A minister should always have more passion for his wife than he has for anything but God. Sometimes, the minister must put aside the duties and actions of ministry and concentrate on loving his wife. The passage in Scripture of Mary and Martha as Jesus visited comes to mind. Martha scrambled around the house performing tasks of "ministry" while Mary sat at Christ's feet loving and listening to him. Martha was upset that Mary was not serving as she was. Christ reminded Martha that while what she was doing was helpful, it was not the best thing. Similarly, ministry couples need to remember that scrambling for tasks is not always the best action to take. Sometimes, the best thing that can be done is to love one another.

Remember Your First Love

After being placed upon the pedestal, pastors can easily fall into the trance of chasing after success in the church culture. Before falling into the trap, most pastors had high aspirations of pursing Christ and His gospel, ministering to people on a basic level and following Him wherever He led. Before the trap was set, it all seemed so simple. Then came the expectations and the internalization of those expectations. As they increased, the view of the pastor was heightened and he worked to maintain his position on the pedestal. He worked to appease the culture through program building, increasing numbers and wearing the mask of success. In time, he easily forgot his first love – pursuing Christ and making disciples.

Thousands of books are written each year on the topic of church growth, visitation programs and how to be a successful minister. Every month, it seems, someone has a brand new idea on how to revitalize the church and put people in the pews. Frustrated pastors who have lost their first love often turn to programs to find success in the community and drive up numbers. They slowly turn away from Christ and His people and toward ideas and prepackaged programs.

Could it be as easy as the early church did it? After Pentecost, Peter preached and the church grew. But the pivotal verse is in Acts 2:47: "And the Lord added to their number day by day those who were being saved." The early church was a community of faith, trusting in Christ to do what He wanted in His church. No programs existed to grow the church, certainly, but they were following the example of the disciples and their teaching.

Prevention Tips For Pastors

Counselor Bill Leonard gives four practical prevention tips for pastors:

Endeavor for very strong disciplines: Read God's Word for yourself and let it speak to you. Talk *and* listen to God.

Cultivate your marriage: Know who you are as a man. Have blessed sex with your wife, emotionally, spiritually and intimately.

Find fun things to do not connected to church: Find a hobby, go fishing, walking, bike riding. Do something active to get a strong endorphin release.

Take sabbaticals: Everyone needs time away from work to refocus.

Be careful with your stress levels: Critical stress causes us to distort things like depression and reality.

Programs are not all bad, but when they take the place of chasing after Christ and Christ alone, they become an idol.

Many of the fallen pastors realized they were chasing after ministry more than a relationship with God. Jake Larson noted how the dangerous difference between chasing Christ and chasing ministry:

> *"The number one problem for pastors is that we're chasing after the wrong thing. We should be in ministry because we love Christ, but we're chasing after success. The pressure to be successful is the way we measure things. How many butts are in the seats, how big is our budget and how happy people are with what we're doing. I think that produces a nightmare."*[81]

When ministers begin chasing after ministry for the wrong reasons, it builds pride, and when a pastor becomes prideful, he comes in danger of falling. It is a good reminder in Jesus' parable of the two builders when he speaks of the two men who build on two different types of foundation. One builds his home on sand and the other on rock. The one who builds his house on the sand, his house is devastated. Similarly, when the pastor begins to chase after than anything but the teaching and love of Christ, his fate will be the same when trials come:

> "And the rain fell, and the floods came, and the winds blew
> and beat against that house, and it fell, and great was the
> fall of it."[82]

One way the culture can be changed is by continually placing Christ as the center of the church. Pastors are not the only ones guilty of chasing ministry instead of Christ. Unfortunately, there seems to be a love of church more than love of Christ. Some congregants find pride not in the God they serve, but in the building where they worship. The Bible warns all Christians to have a healthy fear not of the church, but of God. Paul reminded the church of Corinth that they were ultimately weak and had no place to boast before God for anything they accomplished or because of a building they have built:

> "For consider your calling, brothers: not many of you were
> wise according to worldly standards, not many were
> powerful, not many were of noble birth. But God chose what
> is foolish in the world to shame the wise; God chose what is
> weak in the world to shame the strong; God chose what is
> low and despised in the world, even things that are not, to
> bring to nothing things that are, so that no human being
> might boast in the presence of God."[83]

Humility is key for the pastor seeking a right relationship before God. This humility has to be practiced not just before God but towards other people and to one's family. It is not to be lived out as a result of the command of God, but because of a loving desire to serve others and see them as greater than one's self. Wilson and Hoffman encourage the minister to seek humility to avoid being placed on a pedestal and to avoid places of pride. They use Peter's restoration by Christ as an example of humility and a way that he was able to lay aside his "god complex" to be a better servant:

> "A humble understanding of ourselves is necessary to have
> a right view of our calling as ministers. Such understanding

will prevent us from performing for the crowd and instead
encourage us to play to an audience of One. Only then can
we help the sheep entrusted to us to see our proper role in
their lives and encourage them to keep their gaze on God,
their true Shepherd and King." [84]

The church can also help the pastor and themselves by moving away from the idea of church as "the building" and more as the biblical reality of the community of faith. When most Christians are asked what church is, they will predictably point to a building. When some refer to those in the church, they refer to it as "the church family." The point is taken but we are told in Scripture instructs that Christ is head of the church. When the church is perceived as a building, Christ is seemingly left out on Sunday instead of the community enjoying His presence as He is pursued daily.

This is not a new idea in Scripture. When God gave Israel the command to love Him with all their heart, soul and might,[85] he also gave them another command. He told them that those words would be on their heart. He said to teach it to their children, to talk about it every chance they got and to write it down in places where they would be constantly reminded of it and of Him. God was telling the Israelites how important community was, but more importantly, of His place within the community as they worshipped all week long as they lived, remembering God together.

Know and Admit Your Strengths and Weaknesses

The statistics prove it and the pastors who were interviewed confirmed it. Pastors are under an extreme amount of stress and have exceedingly high expectations placed upon them. This does not always lead to moral failure, but more often leads to depression, anxiety and burnout. The pastor must understand who he is and know his limitations. Besides being a fallen creature, there is a reason each pastor sins in the first place. Ministers have a set of strengths that God gifted him or her with to lead their congregation. Each minister also has a set of weaknesses that need to be identified so they will not repeat the same mistakes. Pastors are often quick to take credit for their strengths, but may not be as quick to recognize their weaknesses. Ministers are weak, fallible humans capable of sin and need to be able to take account of every part of their emotional being. Counselor Bill Leonard shared the following:

> "You have to try to stay in realistic expectations. We're not omni-anything. We're not celestial, we're not angelic, we're human beings. We have talents, gifts, anointing, all that, but we're just human beings. And all these human beings we read about in Scripture, even Jesus Son of God in Gethsemane, experienced grief emotions, showing us His humanness."[86]

There are many good tools for pastors to evaluate their strengths including one by Ministry Insights. Rodney Cox explains that a pastor must learn to lead from his strengths and allow people to surround him to help him in his weaknesses:

> "Each of us brings a set of strengths to any role. What we see is a lot of pastors journey after things God didn't give them and become something God didn't create them to be. What that does is isolate them."[87]

When isolation occurs, it can set the pastor up for a fall in different areas of his life. The pastor then looks for ways to make up for that loneliness elsewhere as Cox explains:

> "In that isolation they become shifted. You're isolated from your church, your wife. You're basically alone on an island. You're basically looking to have fellowship somewhere. You're looking for a way to do what we were designed to do and that's to have a relationship."[88]

There does exist in the church culture an expectation for the pastor to be superhuman. On one hand, many members hold the pastor in high regard due to his position. That regard is dangerous when he becomes elevated to the place of idol and he is seen to have no weaknesses whatsoever. He becomes a man void of moral, personal or ideological weakness and when he does make a mistake, he can become quickly vilified.

On the other hand, the pastor can buy into the perception of his indestructibility. He may think he has to live up to how others perceive him.

He knows he is weak, but strives to conceal his weaknesses. He steps into church each Sunday, putting on his best church face and plays the best pastor role he can, despite knowing the wretchedness in his heart.

Again, the church culture needs reformation. In this case, the church has placed a weak man in the place of perfect idol. The idol who accepts these accolades is a knowing hypocrite and as time goes on, he becomes more and more frustrated with the distance between reality and fantasy. What can be done to change the culture?

One time, Jesus caught the disciples arguing about what prominent place they'd have in the kingdom once He took over. He didn't care for that. Another time, Peter began to brag about wanting to suffer for Jesus. Jesus basically told Him, "Oh, you will suffer for me. Just like me." Those in ministry have high and lofty ideals for where they want to go, where they want to be and sometimes, how they want to look.

But Jesus will have none of that. He called a bunch of smelly fishermen and He never asked them to try and be anything different under their own power. He just said, "Follow me." He promised them His power. Yes, He did tell them to take up their crosses and deny themselves. But one thing He did not do was tell them to chase after the job. He didn't tell them the key to a successful Day of Pentecost was busting their tails, prioritizing their committee action reports and making sure everyone was right on schedule. God did it all.

Changing the culture begins by relying on God and not on ourselves. This does not mean laying back and doing nothing. Our expectations of ourselves are too high and our expectations of God are too low. The statistics tell us that pastors are spending 60 hours a week in the office overworking themselves in the tasks of ministry and I wonder how much of it is necessary. We have the mantra of, "If I don't do it, it won't get done," or "If I don't do it, someone will be mad at me." Many pastors have forgotten to pursue Christ as head of the church. He promised to do all the heavy lifting. Meanwhile, pastors are stressing themselves out, taking anti-anxiety medication and trusting in their own power while their physical and mental health crumbles.

Christ is the power unto salvation and only through Him do we find life and power for ministry. As pastors, we must lower our expectations of ourselves. We are not going to change the world under our power, from our pulpit, by our preaching. Pastors aren't going to change the world by extending the number of hours we work, by paying more attention to that complaining member, by skipping our vacation every year to appease the church or by pushing themselves further than they know they should be pushed.

> *Pastors need to let their churches know how weak we are. This is a terrifying thought for most pastors. They are not able to do everything. However, deep down, pastors want their churches to think they can do everything. They want them to think that they are able to solve everyone's problems through counseling, preach amazing messages, visit every elderly person in the church every week, pray for four hours every morning, teach Sunday School, be available in their office all day, love every dish they cook for potluck and are content with the salary they provide for them. It's not the truth. Most pastors are worn out, unhappy people.*

Pastors love to tell people that we are content in Christ, but ministers are either dropping like flies or they're sending out resumes. The solution is to be as honest as possible with your church. Be loving, be caring, present your case as a real human being. Don't be afraid to post office hours and tell them that you can't do it all. Don't be afraid to tell them that the deacon or elder body needs to step up more. Don't be afraid to share how broken you are in your current situation. Tell them it's not about wanting a raise or a sabbatical or a few weeks off, but about being a better pastor with realistic expectations. But don't let yourself die a slow, horrible, miserable death in the ministry. Christ called us to be a healthy body, producing members with joy for His sake.

Be honest with your church. Remind them of the mission of the church body and the community of faith. If you need help, show them the statistics in this book. Bring in an older pastor who knows the wisdom of lowering expectations. Bring in an expert from your denomination to share with them ways to work together as a body of Christ to support you and be fully functional. Show them specific details of your schedule and the visits you make and the hours you spend doing the tasks of ministry. Whatever you do, don't delay. Do it for your sake, for your children's sake, for your marriage's sake and for your future.

Summary

There is a way to prevent ministry failure and it begins with the pastor being able to be real within the fellowship in which he serves. He and his wife must never feel constraint to communicate physically, emotionally or spiritually. Anything that would come between them should be seen as a threat and monitored closely. Transparency between them will always serve as an accountability tool. Besides always focusing on his wife, he should always remember that ministry is not about a task, but about pursuing the person of Jesus Christ. Finally, knowing one's strengths and weaknesses is essential in preventing a fall.

God does not want those He calls to fail. He has given them resources beyond belief by His Word and Spirit. There are warnings throughout Scripture about ministry failure as well as many books on the evangelical market. What is most important is that pastors remain humble enough to realize that a fall is just moments away when their eyes are not upon Christ. So much is at stake for the minister and it is easy to become overwhelmed by the pressure. However, we must also remember the loving statement made by the One who called us:

> "Come to me all who labor and are heavy laden, and I will
> give you rest. Take my yoke upon you, and learn from me, for
> I am gentle and lowly in heart, and you will find rest for your
> souls. For my yoke is easy, and my burden is light."[89]

Chapter 21

Changing The Culture

The church culture is desperately ill. It has a disease that produces pastors who are jumping ship from the ministry, some into adultery. The process of this disease repeats itself continually in churches across the country. The church hires a pastor who is given a set of expectations for his ministry. He receives appreciation and accolades from the church which internally flame his own expectations. He works harder to meet the expectations and spends more time and energy chasing after the ministry than he does at home. The church shifts their appreciation to a sort of idolatry for him. He is seen as more than a man and placed on a pedestal. As the expectations grow, his stress increases.

The pastor is part of this sick church culture as well, one that leads to his own downfall. He begins to chase after the impossible task of meeting impossibly higher demands. The ministry becomes for him a kind of mistress. In turn, his marriage breaks down over time and he pours more time into the church culture. Eventually, some event triggers a disassociation with the church and he begins to need more appreciation. He begins to look elsewhere to meet those needs, usually in some fantasy and eventually in another woman. His sin is eventually discovered and he is immediately dismissed. This is the outcome of the disease that afflicts the church culture.

The result of this disease that is afflicting the church culture gets most of the attention. When a pastor falls, the church typically turns its head and blames the pastor. Unfortunately, treating the outcome does nothing to treat the disease.

The systemic problem is much greater. The church culture is at risk of continually producing fallen pastors unless it can reform itself. Several suggestions have been made in specific areas already, but a step back from the problem might be useful.

One of the continuing conversations within the church is whether the church culture is beyond repair. Some believe the culture is so entrenched with the repeated pattern of failure that to reform every church is an impossible task. The disease has become "business as usual" and to suggest church members enter into any other kind of thinking would be untenable. The only foreseeable alternative is to begin new fellowships with a proper idea of community.

Starting new churches is an excellent idea and a biblical notion. There is a concern that needs to be addressed for starting a new church. Even when a new church is started, human beings are involved. People bring in old types of thinking and may replicate the things they have learned elsewhere. Starting a new church poses its own set of challenges and may not remove the problem of a diseased church culture.

The prospect of reforming existing church cultures is intimidating and overwhelming. Change will take time, patience and leadership willing to be transparent and compassionate. Christ gave us a pattern for this type of change. When He came to proclaim the kingdom, it was a life-changing message that required a change in the ways people were living. He challenged the practices people had set up for their religion. He was bringing to them a message of the heart and not of external practice.

Even when Christianity moved on to the book of Acts, the Jewish Christians had difficulty interacting with the Gentile Christians. The external laws of purity were placed aside and caused argument for many years over which ones to keep. When change is suggested, it takes a long time for people to allow it or to even entertain the idea.

Christ as Culture Changer

The greatest example for a bad culture was the one that surrounded Christ. He was the Messiah, yet people had differing expectations of what the Messiah should be. Many thought He should usurp the Roman authority as a warrior. The culture placed the wrong expectations upon Christ and elevated a false image of what Messiah should be. By doing so, their hopes and expectations were dashed and many rejected His claim to be their deliverer. From this, it can be seen that not all expectations are bad. Those who came to understand Christ as the one who would deliver them from sin had the right expectation. Those who set up false expectations led themselves astray and marred their image of Jesus.

Today's church culture has a similar choice to make. When church leaders are approached, they must move their expectations into line with reality. If pastors are expected to be on call around the clock, preach perfect sermons, visit every sick person in the church, break up every quarrel, increase membership and giving, have a perfect family and perform all these tasks while looking good, he will be set up for a fall and the church will be set up for a disappointment.

Instead, the pastor and church must be transparent with one another about realistic expectations. Every member of the community must be aware of the role of the pastor within that specific fellowship as well as knowing their own role. Each member of the community of faith should know that the pastor and its leaders are people who have strengths and weaknesses. The community of faith can be encouraged to exercise their own gifts to complement the weaknesses of the pastor.

Christ also exercised great humility in his ministry. He deserved to be worshipped and praised and placed above all else. Yet Christ lowered Himself and performed the most humbling acts found in the bible. The expectations placed upon Him were great and the pressure was tremendous, but Christ repeatedly lowered Himself. He went out of His way to associate with the outcasts of society. He washed His disciple's feet, which was the job of a servant. His most humbling act was His supreme sacrifice at Calvary.

It is easy to place church leaders upon a pedestal and into the place of an idol. Many pastors show great charisma and combine that with a gift for preaching and a love for people. When that admiration for them turns into idolatry, the trap is set. Christ's constant example of humility is one to be constantly remembered. If anyone ever had the right to step foot on this earth and be worshipped, it was Him. Yet Christ did not actively seek praise, admiration or worship. He constantly moved toward people who needed compassion.

It is a good thing to show appreciation to a pastor, but when it crosses the line, it becomes dangerous. The pastor's ego can feed off of praise and fall into a dangerous cycle. The best thing for a pastor is to practice humility. The greater the accolades and praise, the more humble one should seek to be.

Christ showed another way to change the culture. As soon as His public ministry began, He sought out disciples. His ultimate purpose was to train them and teach them to carry out the plan for the church. But Christ also had twelve men with whom He walked daily and shared His life with. When these men began the church in Acts, they did so with a strong sense of community.

Today's culture appears to be disjointed in comparison to the early church. Pastors do not have many close friends while in the ministry. Church is often viewed as a building to worship in rather than a community of believers that exists outside the four walls. Christ intentionally put time into building relationships with his disciples. Many pastors are wary of building relationships with people in their church because they are afraid of being burned. It is important to remember that several times his disciples let Him down. Christ wasn't concerned with how relationships would turn out. He was interested in building people up and investing in their lives. There is no substitute for having people walk together with the pastor, sharing their lives together.

Jesus repeatedly demonstrated two things that are a must for anyone willing to change the culture: patience and prayer. His disciples often seemed slow to get His point while He was teaching. Right up to the cross, they were confused about His mission. Jesus was patient with them and led them through it all in a compassionate manner. He also prayed constantly. With all divine power available to Him in an instant, He never neglected prayer. He taught His followers the necessity of prayer to make changes.

If change is going to occur, it will take time. Church leaders will have to cast a vision and understand the reality of the problem that is causing pastors to fall. Coupled with that, leadership will have to demonstrate great patience and prayer. If change occurs, it will be a work of God in the hearts of His people and leaders. No program or two week bible study will be enough to stop the dangerous cyclical culture that has embedded itself into the church. A heart change is necessary for all those who desire to see the stronghold of ministry failure stop.

Conclusion

Changing a culture is a difficult job, but it's not impossible and it is worth it. To restore a culture is to participate in the kingdom of God. To repent of the idol is to discover life. To launch a new church is life-giving.

My heart breaks for all of the pastors in this book, the churches who were hurt by their fall and the families involved. Those events did not need occur. Each fall is horrifying and awful. Sin is a terrible thing and should concern each believer. I do believe that future ministry failure can be prevented and avoided, but the pastor and church must work together as a community of faith in order for this to happen and for God to be glorified.

Many churches in America tend to look more like businesses than they do authentic spiritual communities, with the pastor as the CEO. He is hired to grow the church, increase the giving, bring in the young people and energize the membership. The expectations placed upon him are often unreachable and unreasonable. However, the pastor agrees to these expectations and trudges forward, to the detriment of his health, family and spirituality.

We are afraid to be authentic with one another. Pastors are afraid to share their weaknesses with their congregants. Instead of telling the church how weak they are, they strive harder to show them how strong they can be. In doing so, they give a false image of greatness that has already been cultivated throughout the generations by the church. The idolized pastor, who can do no wrong, who can do everything becomes an icon and not a real man.

Scripture calls us to be a body of people, striving to be least among one another, having a God assigned role and looking to Christ as the head of the church. What we need to remember is that all of us are fallen people, capable of the most awful sin, yet forgiven in spite of what we've done. We are a church full of sinners forgiven by God, overlooking the faults of others and supportive and gracious to those who do fall.

Appendix A

Quick Answers for Emergency Situations

This book offers a long term solution to a problem that has existed in the church culture for decades. Still, there are those who are looking for a quick crutch when a fracture has taken place. Answers are needed immediately in our world when time is pressing and people are scrambling for life to make sense. There is no substitute for reading this entire book, but I would like to give a brief help for those who might be seeking emergency room type help for a situation that needs lengthy surgery.

A serious note needs to be made when it comes to fallen pastors, moral failure and the churches that are affected – there are no quick answers. There is no band-aid big enough to cover the horrible gash left behind when a pastor betrays his family, church, friends and his God. That is why this book exists. But healing is possible.

I'm a Fallen Pastor and I Just Got Caught! What Do I Do?

Don't hide your sin. Confess it to those who lead over you. The best thing you can do is find a friend in ministry to stand by you as you face the people you have disappointed greatly. Seek restoration with your wife and above all else, know that you are in for a long road ahead. Do not forget that despite your sin, you are greatly loved by Christ and His forgiveness is readily available for you.

I'm a Fallen Pastor and It's Been a Few Months and I Still Don't Have Peace

You're going through a long process that takes time. The last couple of chapters deal with that, but don't skip right to them. It is a long road that leads to repentance. Don't expect overnight results after a sin that devastated you and many around you. Seek out those things you loved first – your wife, your faith and your God. Surround yourself with people who will hold you accountable and help you change.

Help! We Just Found Out Our Pastor Was Committing Moral Sin!

Don't move too quickly. Does he need to be removed from the pulpit? Yes. But do nothing out of anger. Consult your local association (if you have one) or local church counselors before you move. Remember that, despite his sin, he is still your brother in Christ with a family. How you deal with him will ultimately hinge on whether he repents, something that is dealt with in this book. It does hurt, it is disappointing, but don't do anything that would send him or his family down a further destructive path. If you can't handle his situation, find someone who can.

I'm a Pastor and I'm Thinking of Cheating on My Wife

Don't do it. I could write out all the verses about committing adultery, but you already know them. The things you think are true in your mind right now may not be reality. Take the time to read the testimonies in this book. Sin has real consequences. Regardless of how you feel you are being treated in your marriage or church, there is no reason to sin before the face of God.

A Pastor Friend of Mine Cheated – What Should I Do?

Love him like you would want to be loved in that situation. He's the same person he was before you found out, but now he's under the public eye for a sin he committed. He'll be under severe scrutiny and he needs friends now more than ever. He doesn't need judges, he needs people willing to listen, walk with him, occasionally correct him, but most of all he just needs people to understand. It is a difficult thing to choose to associate with a fallen pastor. There are times to listen and times to correct. But if you're his friend, you will know how to discern.

I'm a Pastor Who Knows This Could Happen to Me – What Do I Do?

Read on and protect yourself. Be wary that you remember why you got into the ministry in the first place. You probably didn't get into it because you wanted to have a sanctuary filled with 2,000 people with a full orchestra and four satellite campuses. You probably got into it because you were called by God to love His people. Don't ever forget that.

I'm a Seminary Student Being Forced to Read This Book – This Won't Ever Happen to Me

Be wary of pride. When I entered seminary and had a class on the practice of ministry, I said the same exact thing. I thought I was invincible. I was in love with my wife and knew that the Word of God was strong within my heart. I saw my future before me unfolding and was confident in my preaching, my love of Christ and my character. Read on, my friend.

Appendix B

Resources for Further Help

XXXChurch.com

Throughout the interview process, several pastors mentioned a struggle with pornography. Many pastors fight the temptation of lust and there is an excellent resource available for anyone who is struggling. Jake Larson, who was interviewed for this book, is co-founder of Fireproof Ministries and blogs at XXXChurch.com. Their ministry aids people to be accountable and fight the addiction to pornography. Jake described their ministry in detail:

> *"We started XXXChurch in 2002 because for years we were speaking to youth across the country and we were addressing the issue of pornography before it was popular – it's not really popular still – but before it was acceptable. Now as we've progressed and are ten years old in 2012, we basically do three things: Awareness, prevention and recovery.*
>
> *"We do a ton of awareness. This is happening in your homes. It's invading every home in America. It's leading to other sins: Child pornography, adultery, fantasy life, breaking apart jobs and people are spending entire days looking at porn. And in recovery and on the prevention side of things, we do software and online accountability programs. Online accountability is glasslike in the way it's produced. When someone uses our X3 Watch or X3 Watch PRO, a filter and online accountability program, it will immediately text message your accountability partner the inappropriate content you just looked at online. That's probably the main thing we've said with our ministry, we've said 'Porn's the dirty little secret because it's something you don't talk about*

and that dirty little secret is destroying us because we don't talk about it and we aren't honest about it.' So we thought, 'How can we help with prevention?'

"In recovery, we have online workshops, 30 day workshops for adults, for singles, for married couples on the issue of pornography of 15 sessions that teach with books and resources that are available. Not just to say, 'Oh, I have a problem,' but to say, 'Why do I have a problem, and what's the source? What are the triggers and why am I walking down this journey and how can I get out? How can I make wise decisions in the future?'"

Preventing Ministry Failure: A ShepherdCare Guide for Pastors, Ministers and Other Caregivers, by Michael Todd Wilson and Brad Hoffmann

This book is a practical, preventative guide for ministers. It examines some of the same cultural issues discussed in this book and others. It is a personal guide for ministers to work through some of the problems they might encounter before they happen. It aids the pastor in setting up boundaries in his ministry as well as developing good people skills.

The Leading From Your Strengths Profile

This tool will give you an opportunity to move the concepts outlined in this appendix from theory to application. While we have spoken broadly here about differences, in less than 10 minutes you can become far more specific. The Leading From Your Strengths Profile is a 24-page report on your individual and relational strengths that is generated from an online assessment that is completed in only 8-10 minutes; your personal results will then be provided immediately.

The Profile is packed full of valuable insights and information that will help identify your strengths and those of your team, spouse and children to clearly identify your differences. On the basis of your individual Profile data, and the teaching in this appendix, a dialogue can be initiated to help move you toward blending your differences to produce what God intended: unity and oneness in your relationship.

For pricing information, and to complete the Leading From Your Strengths Profile, go to www.leadingfromyourstrengths.com. I have also given you a discount coupon below that you can apply at time of checkout.

Discount Coupon: raycarroll

Appendix C

Questions for Discussion

Chapter 2 - Ray

1. What role did personal tragedy play in Ray's fall?

2. How would you counsel someone who had tragedy in their life as they dealt with temptation?

Chapter 3 - Kris

1. How did Kris' fall change his ego?

2. What actions could Kris have taken to bolster his personal accountability before his fall?

Chapter 4 – Paul

1. What can be learned from Paul's halting his relationship with Marleigh before it crossed into the physical?

2. The church seemed to be content to sweep Paul's sin under the rug. Were the reasons they gave valid? Is there ever a good reason to hide sin from the church?

Chapter 5 – Dathan

1. How could Dathan have overcome the church's doubts about his repentance?

2. What are some ways an outside church can reach out to a fallen pastor effectively?

Chapter 6 – Shannon

1. Like other fallen pastors, Shannon reported finding only one friend who would talk to him after his fall. What are some reasons people would choose to reject the fallen minister and some would choose to stand by him regardless of his sin?

Chapter 7 – Dominic

1. Dominic reached out to his leadership team when he recognized he might be in danger, but they did not understand his problem. What might be an effective way for an exhausted pastor to effectively communicate his problem to church leadership before a fall occurs?

2. Dominic noted many of the excessively high expectations that had been placed on him. What are some of the unrealistic expectations churches place on pastors? What are some expectations that pastors feel are high but may not be?

Chapter 8 – Lance

1. How much did Lance's stress seem to affect his fall?

2. Lance and Kari sought restoration as a newly married couple. Many people probably had a problem with this. How would you handle this?

Chapter 9 – Vincent

1. Many of Vincent's former church members left his former church because they were disillusioned with his sin or disappointed with the way the church handled his dismissal. How can someone minister to a church member under such stress?

Chapter 10 – Gary

1. At the end of his story, Gary reflected upon a fallen pastor who committed suicide months after his fall. The story reminds us that pastors are human and even in their sin, their falls leave them hurt and broken. What role can empathy play for those who might decide to reach out to a fallen pastor?

Chapter 11 – Denny

1. Denny had hopes and aspirations beyond being a pastor yet kept putting them aside for the goals and desires of the church. How might this have attributed to his fall?

2. Denny spoke of guilt and shame when he went into public after his fall, a common experience of many fallen pastors. What might be a

proper response to seeing a fallen pastor in public shortly after his fall?

Chapter 12 – Joe

1. Like Joe's story, most fallen pastor's stories are complex, filled with difficult problems. Joe was in a tempting situation after his wife was found to be cheating on him. How would you walk beside Joe during this process?

2. Joe was able to minister to other fallen pastors. Why would Joe be a good candidate to minister in this area?

Chapter 13- Josh

1. As with many stories of fallen pastors, Josh found himself in a place where he was experiencing humbling circumstances but was not humbled. Why don't humbling circumstances always bring humility?

Endnotes

1   Ray Carroll. Interview with Hershael York. Phone interview, May 9, 2011.

2   Ray Carroll. Interview with Bill Leonard. Phone interview, May 4, 2011.

3   Richard J. Krejcir "Statistics on Pastors: What is Going on with the Pastors in America?," Francis Schaeffer Institute of Church Leadership, 2006, http://www.intothyword.org/apps/articles/default.asp?articleid=36562, accessed 10/11/12.

4   James Dobson, Focus on the Family Newsletter, "The Titanic, The Church: What They Have in Common," August, 1998.

5   Krejcir.

6   Tina Dirmann, "Pastoral Pressures Test Faith." Los Angeles Times, 1/29/99, accessed online 5/8/11.

7   Leadership, Fall 1992, "Marriage Problems Pastors Face"

8   Fuller Institute of Church Growth, "1991 Survey of Pastors," (Pasadena, CA: Fuller Theological Seminary, 1991). from H. B. London, Jr. and Neil B. Wiseman, "Pastors at Risk," Victor Books, 1993, p. 22.

9   Michael Todd Wilson & Brad Hoffmann, Preventing Ministry Failure: A ShepherdCare Guide for Pastors, Ministers and Other Caregivers, (Downers Grove, IL: InterVarsity Press, 2007), 17.

10   Ibid, 18.

11   Barna Group, "A Profile of Protestant Pastors in Anticipation of 'Pastor Appreciation Month'," September 25, 2001, http://www.barna.org/barna-update/article/5-barna-update/59-a-profile-of-protestant-pastors-in-anticipation-of-qpastor-appreciation-month (accessed 9/25/01).

12   Fuller.

13   Ray Carroll. Interview with Mark D. Roberts. Phone interview, July 30, 2011.

14   Krejcir

15   Ray Carroll. Interview with Jake Larson. Phone interview, August 12, 2011.

16   Barna Group, "Many Churchgoers and Faith Leaders Struggle to Define Spiritual Maturity," May 11, 2009, http://www.barna.org/barna-update/article/5-barna-update/59-a-profile-of-protestant-pastors-in-anticipation-of-qpastor-appreciation-month (accessed 5/11/01).

17   Leonard, interview.

18   York, interview.

19   Ray Carroll. Interview with Steve Reed. Phone interview, April 19, 2011.

20   1 Corinthians 9:22.

21   Ray Carroll. Interview with Rodney Cox. Phone interview, April 26, 2011.

22   Leonard, interview.

23   Krejeir.

24   Cox, interview.

25   Ray Carroll. Interview with Troy Haas. Phone interview, May 4, 2011.

26   Fuller.

27   Barna Group, "Pastors Feel Confident in Ministry, But Many Struggle in Their Interaction With Others," July 10, 2006, http://www.barna.org/barna-update/article/17-leadership/150-pastors-feel-confident-in-ministry-but-many-truggle-in-their-interaction-with-others?q=generational+differences (accessed 9/24/11).

28   Barna Group, "Surveys Show Pastors Claim Congregants Are Deeply Committed to God but Congregants Deny It!," January 1, 2006, http://www.barna.org/barna-update/article/5-barna-update/165-surveys-show-pastors-claim-congregants-are-deeply-committed-to-god-but-congregants-deny-it (accessed 9/24/11).

29   Larson, interview.

30   Roberts, interview.

31   Ibid.

32   Cox, interview.

33   Haas, interview.

34   Ibid.

35   Ibid.

36   Leonard, interview.

37   York, interview.

38   Larson, interview.

39   Ibid.

40   Ibid.

41   Leadership Journal, "The Leadership Survey on Pastors and Internet Pornography," 1/1/01, http://www.christianitytoday.com/le/2001/winter/12.89.html (accessed 8/18/11).

42   Larson, interview.

43   Kailla Edger, Losing the Bond With God: Sexual Addiction and Evangelical Men (Santa Barbara: Praeger, 2011), 67.

44   Ibid, 97.

45   Larson, interview.

46   David Trotter, Lost and Found: Finding Myself by Getting Lost in an Affair (Charleston, South Carolina: Nurmal, 2010).

47   Ray Carroll. Interview with David Trotter. Phone interview, August 10, 2011.

48   Trotter, interview.

49   York, interview.

50   Job 1:21.

51   Earl Wilson, Steering Clear: Avoiding the Slippery Slope to Moral Failure (Downers Grove: InterVarsity Press, 2002), 85-6.

52   Wilson, Restoring, 60.

53   York, interview.

54   Wilson, Steering, 101.

55   Ibid, 51.

56   York, interview.

57   Ibid.

58   Ibid.

59   Ibid.

60   Ibid.

61   Ibid.

62   Ibid.

63   Roberts, interview.

64   Wilson, Restoring, 126.

65   Ibid.

66   York, interview.

67   Ray Carroll. Interview with Roger Barrier. Phone interview, April 12, 2011.

68   Earl & Sandy Wilson, et. al., Restoring the Fallen: A Team Approach to Caring, Confronting & Reconciling (Downers Grove: InterVarsity Press, 1997), 22.

69   Psalm 51:4.

70   Wilson, Restoring, 44-5.

71   Wilson, Restoring, 118.

72   Haas, interview.

73   Ibid.

74   Edger, 107.

75   Wilson, Steering, 138.

76   Ephesians 5:25.

77   Leonard, interview.

78   York, interview.

79   Trotter, interview.

80   Roberts, interview.

81   Larson, interview.

82   Matthew 7:27.

83   1 Corinthians 1:26-29, ESV.

84   Wilson, Ministry Failure, 20.

85   Deuteronomy 6:5.

86   Leonard, interview.

87   Cox, interview.

88   Ibid.

89   Matthew 11:28-30, ESV.

Made in the USA
Charleston, SC
28 December 2011